Souvenirs

David Zwirner Books

ekphrasis

Souvenirs
From a Memoir
Élisabeth Louise Vigée Le Brun

Introduction by Anne Higonnet

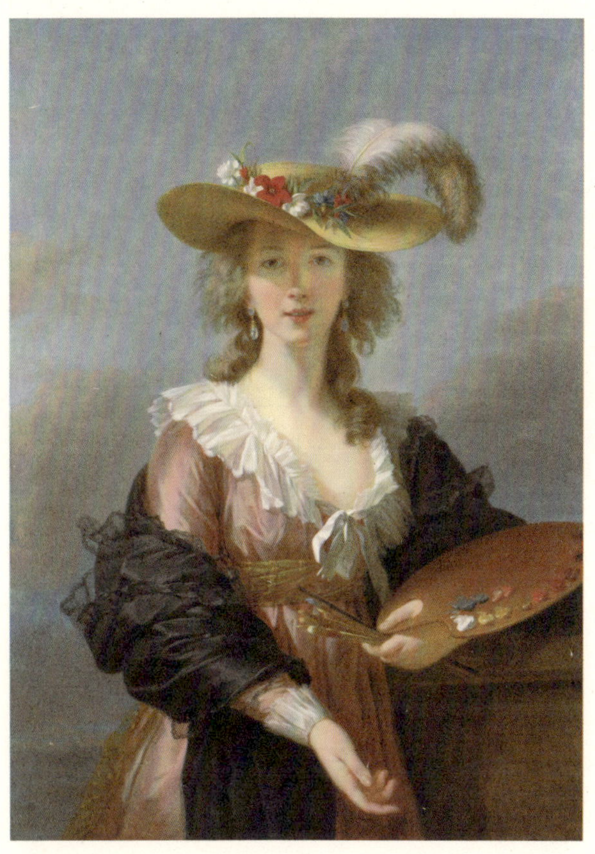

Élisabeth Louise Vigée Le Brun, *Self-Portrait in a Straw Hat*, 1782.
Oil on canvas, 38 ½ × 27 ¾ inches | 97.8 × 70.5 cm

Introduction

Anne Higonnet

When the memoirs of Élisabeth Louise Vigée Le Brun, first published in 1835, were republished in 1984, it was an art-history event.[1] The book cover announced, "Une edition féministe de Claudine Herrmann." So did the reputation of the publisher, boldly named Des Femmes. As a graduate student awakened by the 1980s movement for the inclusion of women in the arts, I rushed to the Des Femmes bookstore in Paris and devoured Vigée Le Brun's pages.

Between her birth in 1755 and her death in 1842, Vigée Le Brun conducted a spectacularly successful painting career. By the age of fifteen she had become professional, by seventeen famous, by her early twenties the official portraitist of Marie Antoinette, Queen of France. In 1776, she married a prominent paintings dealer, Jean-Baptiste-Pierre Le Brun, with whom she had a daughter, Jeanne Julie Louise. Vigée Le Brun worked ceaselessly, doing as many as three portrait sittings a day, she said. She also said that she kept painting while in labor, between contractions. By the end of her life, she had authored more than eight hundred works of art. Her portraits commanded four thousand to twelve thousand francs[2] at a time when almost all professionals were men and had incomes of about one to three thousand francs a year.[3] Her husband was legally entitled to her income, and he gambled most of it away. Vigée Le Brun claimed to have earned a million francs by 1792, when she fled France to escape the Revolution and left her husband. The nobility of Europe clamored for her portraits; she found lucrative work in Italy, Germany, Austria, England, and imperial Russia.

Here is the story of the first modern woman artist who was acclaimed in her own lifetime and made a fortune, who projected a feminine artistic authority in self-portraits, and who lived through the world-historical upheavals of the French Revolution of 1789, the Napoleonic era, and the restoration of monarchy. She had so much confidence in the importance of her career that she created a narrative version of it by writing the *Souvenirs*, which, she said, would "double" her existence.

Vigée Le Brun's *Souvenirs* itself contains two stories, one of them always considered epic, the other once considered curious. The epic charts a rebellion against monarchy, the first declaration of the rights of man, and Europe plunged into political maelstrom; the curiosity records the life of an anomalous, if charming, portrait painter who succeeded in a profession almost entirely closed to women.

Among periods that attract attention to contemporaneous memoirs, the era of the French Revolution—the last quarter of the eighteenth century through about 1830—ranks high. Readers have been fascinated by how the Revolution's forces were felt by individuals, especially those who, like Vigée Le Brun, knew many of its prominent characters. Did people anticipate such a momentous change? Can personal experiences clarify the Revolution's bewilderingly dense and rapidly reversing phases—the constitutional phase of 1789–1792; the arbitrary violence of the 1792–1794 Terror; the 1794–1799 Directory reaction against the Terror; the 1799–1804 Consulate rise of Napoleon to power; the Napoleonic Empire and wars of 1804–1815; and the 1815 restoration of French monarchy? All memoirs craft interpretations of the past, none more so than those that purport to record the French Revolution.

Every memoir of the revolutionary era has to be read through the lens of the political position the writer took after the events of that era. Authors' accounts of each of the Revolution's phases depend on their retrospective position, which means that their memoirs must be read skeptically and contextually. Vigée Le Brun wrote her memoirs convinced that the whole Revolution had been a horrible error, which ended with the relief of monarchy reinstated. Hence her repeated shudders at the memory of the Terror. You would never know, if you took her *Souvenirs* at face value, that at the ideological heart of the Revolution was the principle of equal rights for all human beings. You would not guess that revolutionaries acted on their ideals of an elected government, the abolition of slavery, the introduction of rights for women, the enfranchisement of Jews, and the tolerance of homosexuality. Admittedly, none of these dreams were fully put into practice before the Revolution ended, which made them harder to discern.

After 1984, the story within the *Souvenirs* that had been a curiosity began to feel epic too. Herrmann's edition reached back to the 1869 French edition, which preserved key features of Vigée Le Brun's own composition. Herrmann, however, cut from the original title page an epigraph from Jean-Jacques Rousseau and a sprawling list of institutional honors: "de l'Académie Royale de Paris, de Rouen, de Saint-Luc, de Rome, et d'Arcadie, de Parme et de Bologne, de Saint-Pétersbourg, de Berlin, de Genève et Avignon." And Herrmann rejected the 1894 French edition sweetened and abridged for girls by Amélie Bouvet Carette, which Lionel Strachey used as the basis for his further altered and translated 1903 edition.

Unfortunately, all too many English readers have relied on the many reprintings of the Strachey version, some of them even further abridged. In its full French version, Vigée Le Brun's tale of irrepressible genius matches the combative masculinist prowess of Benvenuto Cellini's revered, legendary *Autobiography*—but in a radically different mode. Cellini's memoir, composed between about 1558 and 1562 but published only in 1728, supplied the norm, Vigée Le Brun's the retort. According to her narrative, she glided straight into social, financial, artistic, and institutional success, at the same time that her appearance was complimented and her maternity approved.

Vigée Le Brun framed her narrative with her relationships to other women. She called the first sections of the *Souvenirs* "letters," not chapters—letters addressed to the prominent musician, the Princess Natalia Ivanova Kurakin. Vigée Le Brun's first sentence cast her authorship as a personal response: "My dear good friend—you wish me so very much to write you my Souvenirs that I will no longer refrain from satisfying you." She ended her remembrances with the satisfaction of sharing her last years with her artist nieces, Caroline Vigée de Rivière and Eugénie Le Brun Tripier Le Franc: "They both are become my children, their care and devotion throw a charm over my existence, and it is near these beloved creatures and the friends who are still left to me that I hope to end peacefully a wandering but quiet life, laborious certainly, but honorable." Well, that was not actually "the end" of the original *Souvenirs*. After thirty-eight astringent pen portraits, or "portraits à la plume," Vigée Le Brun's final words consisted of a totally professional, technical last section called "Advice on the Painting of Portraits" (unless you count her list of the paintings she had made over the course of her career).

Vigée Le Brun made her strongest claims to genius, and her fiercest defenses against those who doubted her genius, through the words of others. In the early twenty-first century, we might call her tactic humblebragging.[4]

The announcement that she would double her existence by writing her memoir was couched as the epigraph from Jean-Jacques Rousseau. To open her text, she quoted a poem written by her brother proclaiming her "rare gifts of genius" that put her on "the bold road that leads to immortality."[5] To justify her bid for admission into the exclusive Académie royale de peinture et de sculpture, and its *Salon* exhibition, she included a brash assertion—from an anonymous couplet sent to her—that her "triumphant art" deserved to hang "in the light" at the *Salon*.[6] She confronted the conviction that all genius was fundamentally masculine with a poem by Le Brun-Pindare, worth citing in full as a measure of what she was up against:

Dear Le Brun, Glory brings tempests in its wake;
Envy is ever watchful for talent;
All that which pleases, which merits praise
Must suffer this monster's lies.
Who more than you has been so unjustly plagued?
A manly brush adorns your paintings.
Thou art not praised for thy womanhood:
Yet their just envy and its unrelenting cries
And the serpents unleashed against you
Proclaim better than our tongues how great a man
you are.[7]

Her most extravagant boast of all came in the form of another anonymous poem she said just happened to come her way. It compared her ability to endow inanimate objects with "a soul" to the divine power of Allah.[8] Suggestions that great artists wield a power comparable to a god's had been made for centuries, but normally about men, such as Cellini, not women. Vigée Le Brun's bid came in the context of an unusually long account of her making of a portrait of Muhammad Dervish Kahn, ambassador to the royal court from Tipu Sultan of Mysore, in 1788. Despite the account's detail, it does not make apparent why this portrait warranted its stellar role in the *Souvenirs*. Furthermore, the portrait had disappeared from public view until a major exhibition in 2004, leaving readers in the dark. When the portrait was rediscovered, however, it turned out to indeed be an exceptional painting by an exceptional author known primarily for half-length portraits of pretty white women. A majestic full-length portrait of a man, it is also an extraordinarily respectful, dignified—and rare—image by a white person of someone Indian.

No wonder Vigée Le Brun felt entitled, a few letters later, to present herself as the sublime pride of France, though reminding the Princess Kurakin "that they are the words of a poet":

> O heavenly Le Brun! Pride of France
> Whose creative spirit, whose immortal brush,
> Brings both joy and wonder
> And love from the seeds of admiration[9]

To finish off her sequence of poems, Vigée Le Brun chose one dedicated to her that she attributed to Madame de Genlis, and which summed up her case for herself:

> I have described her ways, I have described her life,
> But to paint her we need your color
> And from your enchanting brush

That sweet and shining magic,
My portrait is but a sketch
Yet your genius and skill
Offer us a picture that is perfect.[10]

Vigée Le Brun used poems like stepping stones along the story the *Souvenirs* told. As poems in rhyme, their capitalized titles and short lines stand out from the prose. You can skip from one poem to the next and get the fundamental message of the *Souvenirs*.

Ostensibly being not written by her, and seemingly extraneous, however, the poems were all too tempting for abridgers to eliminate, as were the pseudo-epistolary addresses to Princess Kurakin and to Countess Anna Potocka recounting her voyages in Switzerland in 1808 and 1809. Vigée Le Brun took a risk with her reputation. The tactic and risk still resonate today. What woman has not hesitated to sing her own praises, hoping someone else would do it for her? But what happens if no one does? Or if your translators and editors decide to cut the strongest accolades in your story, on whatever grounds?

Apart from Vigée Le Brun's strategies to at the same time claim and disclaim her genius—quite a trick—what strikes me most, reading the 1984 edition forty years later, is that she did not understand the relationship between her historical and autobiographical stories. It never occurred to her that only the modern individualism fought for in the French Revolution could allow a professional career to a middle-class woman. She was oblivious to the profoundly egalitarian principle of the Revolution, even though her career was its product. She also rejected the modern capitalism that fueled her husband's private art dealing: A description of her London painting studio as a "shop" offended her so much that she wrote an angry denial to its author.

While Vigée Le Brun remained obtuse in some ways, she practiced an aesthetic sort of modern individualism. She knew Enlightenment ideas. She read Jean-Jacques Rousseau avidly and made a pilgrimage to his grave. From Rousseau she retained a delight in nature, which animated her art, but not a critique of power.

Vigée Le Brun perfected a type of portrait that hardly bothered with the signs of hereditary nobility and monarchic hierarchy—the very ones ancien régime portraits were obliged to supply to fulfill their social function. Instead, she painted her subjects, including aristocrats of the highest rank, with the signs of individual personality: bright light colors glowing from within, subjects smiling at the viewer with intimate sensibility, or with eyes gazing upward in self-absorption. She represented her subjects fashionably, in a distinctly new sense, wearing the latest in a revolving series of clothing, accessories, and furniture styles. To describe her success, she wrote: "In a word, I was the fashion."[11] She congratulated herself that the most fashion-forward party she ever threw used studio prop "costumes" she called Greek.[12] For her own daily wear, she favored loose, straight cotton dresses, called chemises, sashed at the waist, in what she believed was opposition to the rigid ancien régime clothing style.

In what was destined to become the most famous of all Vigée Le Brun's portraits, of Marie Antoinette, the artist neglected to represent the Queen adorned with the marks of monarchic authority, as sumptuary regulations decreed. Instead, she blithely presented her as an ordinary person, in an ultra-fashionable chemise. Vigée Le Brun managed in her *Souvenirs* to forget that the public's outrage over her violation of decorum forced the Court to yank the offending 1783 portrait from exhibition and hastily commission a properly regal substitute. The only hint of the problem in the *Souvenirs* came in the list she made of her works, when she called the chemise portrait "La reine Marie-Antoinette avec un chapeau" and referred to its replacement with the impersonal "La Reine en grand habit."[13] Vigée Le Brun ignored how fashion did not impress a queen's divine right to rule over her people; she made Marie Antoinette look like a citizen who could be held accountable for irresponsible waste.

Vigée Le Brun did not think about fashion's realities, whether from a royalist or revolutionary point of view. It simply never occurred to her what amount of taxes, paid by the French people, Marie Antoinette spent on her clothing and portraits. In 1783 the Queen's clothing budget alone was the prerevolutionary equivalent of 120,000 francs. In 1785 she overspent her budget to the tune of 258,002 francs. The sort of woman who labored on the Queen's clothing was lucky to earn more than

300 francs a year. Vigée Le Brun never questioned what women in daily life were obliged to wear underneath their chemises until deep into the Revolution: rigid stays and petticoats that kept them so immobile they amounted to cages. When she returned to a Consulate Paris, encountered a real fashion revolution that freed women's bodies, and met its leaders (whom she called Madame Bonaparte, Madame Tallien, and Madame Récamier), she admired their beauty but did not fathom the difference between a style and daily physical liberation. Nor did she recognize that the raw materials and fabrics of cotton studio costumes, chemise dresses, and shawls were forcibly imported from colonized India and Kashmir, or that chemises were originally "goles" styled by women of color, many of them enslaved, on brutally colonized Caribbean islands. Like her contemporaries, she gave her fabrics and dresses French names and antique Greek origins, repressing the economic sources of France's wealth.

No wonder Vigée Le Brun was so surprised by the Revolution and by popular resentment against her. Luckily, she was well enough advised to leave France in time to escape the guillotine. And why would she have ceased to be surprised afterward? For the rest of her career, she earned an excellent living wherever she went by painting individualist portraits of the most autocratic nobility in Europe. (The Russian imperial court that embraced her portrait style owned millions of serfs.) The centerpiece of her appeal to her patrons continued to be her relationship with Marie Antoinette. The language of the *Souvenirs* casts the Queen of France almost as a friend, admired and mourned. One of the most striking passages in the whole book occurs when the Queen stoops to pick up a dropped paintbrush for the pregnant artist.

From safely within the realm of high culture, Vigée Le Brun did feel inklings of a desire for equality. It cannot have escaped her notice that one of the very few women inducted with her into the prestigious Académie royale, the only other woman portraitist in her league, Adélaïde Labille-Guiard, supported the Revolution (and survived). Vigée Le Brun routinely praised the talents and achievements of other women artists, ending with the nieces she lived with at the close of her life. She stood up to men in her profession. Her most blistering "portrait à la plume" is of Jacques-Louis David, who dominated the French art world. She called out both his supercilious manners and his merciless betrayal of innocent victims during the Terror.

Nor was Vigée Le Brun incapable of drawing attention to the failings of beautiful women, even when they were protected by the most powerful men. Her "portrait à la plume" of Charles-Maurice de Talleyrand-Périgord, who stayed at the helm of the French government through almost every phase of the era, is devoted mostly to a joke at the expense of his wife: He was fearsomely witty; she was said to be "d'Inde," a pun in French that meant both "from India" and "turkey," meaning "stupid."[14] Vigée Le Brun had painted the portrait of Madame Talleyrand, born Noël Catherine Vorlée, then Madame Grand, in 1783, a painting that is now a treasure of New York's Metropolitan Museum of Art.

Vigée Le Brun came closest to the politics of equality in the artistic domain when she met Germaine de Staël. Vigée Le Brun began her letter, from Switzerland to Countess Potocka, about this encounter by saying she had read Staël's novel *Corinne*. It was tantamount to saying she had read a manifesto in favor of women's potential genius. *Corinne* presented in the palatable form of fiction what Staël campaigned for more abrasively in real life, which is why *Corinne* has inspired great women novelists ever since its publication. Vigée Le Brun then recounted how she posed Staël as her heroine. After a quick list—lyre in hand, rock for a seat, and "costume antique"—she got to the crucial sentence: "Mme de Staël was not exactly pretty, but the liveliness of her features compensated more than adequately for any lack of formal beauty." And then came the alternative to the superficial "beauty" society expected of women: Vigée Le Brun asked Staël to declaim tragic verse so her face would be that of a woman caught in the act of genius. Sure enough, the resulting portrait is a magnificent exception to Vigée Le Brun's pretty pictures of femininity.[15]

Vigée Le Brun's inability to understand the deep connections between history and her autobiography, far from rendering her *Souvenirs* less important, makes it more so. To understand how the French Revolution was torn from within, how successfully it was resisted and reversed, we have to understand how difficult it was at the time both to grasp its central principle and to imagine what the world could be like if that principle were pursued to its logical conclusions. In 2025, we still have trouble imagining what equal rights for every human being means; how can we expect Vigée Le Brun to have been able to in 1835? Furthermore, maybe it was because of, not despite, her inability to perceive all the ramifications and implications of her career that she succeeded so well. A limited but clear goal can focus a mind.

Vigée Le Brun wrote her story as if it were not ordinary but completely normal for a woman artist to move in the most elite circles of society, charge top prices, have praise heaped on her work, reconcile a career with maternity, and look forward to her paintings hanging in the greatest museums in the world. Which is why I still delight in reading the *Souvenirs*. It gives me so much pleasure to read the words of someone who takes for granted that everyone has an equal chance to express their creative spirit.

Notes

1 The editions are as follows: *Souvenirs de Madame Louise-Elisabeth Vigée-Le Brun*. 3 vols. (Paris: Fournier, 1835–1837); *Souvenirs de Mme Vigée Le Brun*, ed. Eugène Fasquelle. 2 vols. (Paris: Charpentier, 1869) (the complete original, with notes by the editor); *Souvenirs of Madame Vigée Le Brun*, rev. Morris F. Tyler (1879; New York: R. Worthington, 1880) (translator unknown; abridged); *Madame Vigée Le Brun*, ed. Amélie Carette (Paris: Paul Ollendorff, 1894) (an edition substantially abridged "pour les jeunes filles"); *Memoirs of Madame Vigée Le Brun*, trans. Lionel Strachey (New York: Doubleday, Page and Company, 1903) ("a rendering of Madame Carette's edition of the Le Brun Memoirs, slightly abridged for the sake of uniformity"); *Souvenirs: Une édition féministe de Claudine Herrmann*. 2 vols. (Paris: Des Femmes, 1984) (a complete reissue of the 1869 Fasquelle edition, minus the title page, with notes by the editor); *The Memoirs of Elisabeth Vigée-Le Brun*, trans. Siân Evans (London: Camden Press, 1989) (a complete translation of the 1984 Herrmann edition, with the reinsertion of the original title page).

2 Herrmann, vol. 1, pp. 91–92.

3 Jean Sgard, "L'Echelle des revenus," *Dix-huitième siècle* 14 (1982): 425–433.

4 For a theorized and psychoanalytic explanation of this tactic, along with a reading list, see Mary D. Sheriff, *The Exceptional Woman: Elisabeth Vigee-Lebrun and the Cultural Politics of Art* (Chicago: The University of Chicago Press, 1996), pp. 6–9, 268.

5 Herrmann, vol. 1, p. 21 (my translation).

6 Herrmann, vol. 1, p. 77 (my translation).

7 Translation from Evans, pp. 44–45.

8 Herrmann, vol. 1, p. 62.

9 Translation from Evans, p. 59.

10 Translation from Evans, p. 300.

11 This volume, p. 53; "en un mot, j'étais à la mode," Herrmann, vol. 1, p. 57.

12 This volume, p. 75; "j'imaginai de nous costumer tous à la grecque," Herrmann, vol. 1, pp. 85–86.

13 Herrmann, vol. 2, p. 340.

14 Herrmann, vol. 2, pp. 313–314.

15 See Sheriff, *The Exceptional Woman*, pp. 239–253. Sheriff makes the case that Vigée Le Brun's portrait of Staël is not only unlike her routinely pretty portraits but also unlike her allegories. Fasquelle in his 1869 edition included a poem written when the portrait was finished (in Paris) by Anne-Marie de Montgeroult, Comtesse de Beaufort d'Hautpoul. This amazingly positive poem likened the painter and the writer, saying, "une même couronne enlace en ce tableau 'Le front inspirateur et l'Immortel pinceau'" ("the same crown encircles this painting 'The Inspiring Mind and the Immortal Brush'"). Herrmann, vol. 2, pp.183–84.

Editor's Note

Élisabeth Louise Vigée Le Brun published her memoirs, her *Souvenirs*, in three volumes during her lifetime, between the years of 1835 and 1837. In 1869, twenty-seven years following her death, they were reissued by Charpentier in Paris, from which subsequent abridgements and translations have been made. This *ekphrasis* volume is a newly abridged edition of the English translation published in 1880 in New York by R. Worthington—a revised and corrected version by Morris F. Tyler of Worthington's 1879 publication of the memoir. The selection here illuminates the life and work of one of the most important modern women artists, focusing on her unique position in the arts as well as her involvement in and views of the social and political dimensions of France and greater Europe in the late eighteenth and early nineteenth centuries.

As the Worthington edition itself abridged passages and omitted select full sections, we have reinstated two examples of the artist's "portraits à la plume" and the pages titled "Advice on the Painting of Portraits," which appeared at the end of the original *Souvenirs* (as they do here). We have also reinserted a letter from Vigée Le Brun sent during her travels in Switzerland for its description of her encounter with the intellectual Germaine de Staël. These sections extend acute insight into Vigée Le Brun's technique and the relationship between revolutionary principles and her own career and status as a woman.

In order to maintain the original character of her memoirs, we have preserved the epistolary structure of the first section of the *Souvenirs*. For the sake of readability, though, we have dispensed with the original numbered chapter headings following the letters to the Princess Kurakin and organized this second section around Vigée Le Brun's travels. We have standardized punctuation and the spellings of identifiable names and places, should readers want to retrace her journey.

Letters to the Princess Kurakin

LETTER I

My dear good friend—you wish me so very much to write you my Souvenirs that I will no longer refrain from satisfying you. What sad feelings will rise within me as I recall the different scenes I have witnessed and the friends who no longer exist, except in my thoughts! However it will not be a difficult task, for my heart remembers well its former friends and in my solitary hours they seem still to be near me, in my imagination.

I will begin by telling you, dear friend, about my childhood and youth, for they foretold my life, since my love for painting developed itself from my earliest years. I was placed in a convent at the age of six; and there I remained till I was eleven. All that time I scribbled everywhere and on everything—my copy books were filled with little heads and profiles; I drew figures and landscapes with charcoal on the walls of the dormitories, and as you can suppose I was often punished for that freak. During my play hours I traced on the sand everything that came into my head. I remember at the age of seven or eight I drew by lamplight a man's head with his beard, which I have always preserved. I showed it to my father, who was extremely pleased and said, "Thou wilt be a painter, my child, if ever there was one."

I tell you all this to show you how innate in me was my love for painting—this love has never decreased; I even believe it has increased with age, for even now I feel the charm of it the same as of yore, and I hope indeed it will not leave me as long as I live. Besides, it is to this divine passion that I am indebted not only for my fortune but my happiness; in my youth, as well as at the present time, it has brought me in contact with the most distinguished and most charming characters in Europe, both men and women. The memory of so many remarkable people gives a great charm to my solitude—I can still see those that are no more, and I am thankful that I have still these visions of a past happiness.

My health in the convent was not very strong, so that my father and mother often came and took me away to spend a few days with them, which was very delightful for me in many ways.

My father, Louis Vigée, drew very well in chalks; there are some portraits of his worthy of La Tour. He also did some oil paintings after Watteau. The one you have seen at my house is rich in coloring and very spirited. But to return to the delights of my father's home, I must tell you that he allowed me to try chalks also, and all day long I used to dabble with his pencils.

He loved his art so much that at times he used to behave in a most eccentric manner. I remember one day he had dressed himself for dining in Paris and had left the house; but remembering a painting which he had just begun he turned back again, to retouch it. He then took off his wig, put on a nightcap, and afterward went out of doors wearing his gold-laced coat and his sword. Had it not been for a kind neighbor who reminded him of his costume, he would have wandered all about the city in that guise.

My father was very witty and clever. His gaiety was so natural that everyone felt inspired with it, too, and very often people came to have their portraits taken on account of his lively conversation and originality. Perhaps you know the following anecdote: One day while he was taking the portrait of a rather pretty woman, he noticed that when he worked at her mouth she kept screwing it up to make it as small as possible. Irritated at last by this trick my father said to her with much calmness: "Don't distress yourself, madame. If you particularly wish it, I can draw you with none at all."

My mother was very beautiful. One can well believe that from the portrait in chalks which my father made of her, as well as from one which I took in oils much later. She was rigidly virtuous. My father adored her like a divinity; but *grisettes* had a great attraction for him.

I was naturally religious and my mother was the same. We always attended the Mass and the everyday services. During Lent we never missed one, not even the evening prayers. Sacred music always had a great influence over me, and the sound of an organ at one time made such an impression on me that I wept without the least idea of why I did so. That sound always reminds me now of my father's death.

In those days my father knew several artists and literary men, who used to come and spend the evening with us. I shall put Doyen at the head, a historical painter, my father's most intimate friend and my first one. Doyen was an excellent man, full of wit and good sense; his ideas about people and things were always very correct;

and he spoke so enthusiastically of painting that he used to make my heart beat with the same feeling. Poinsinet was also very gay and bright; many of his works and plays are still appreciated, and he is the only literary man who ever received three dramatic triumphs in one evening: *Ernelinde*, at the Grand Opéra; *Le Cercle*, at the Française; and *Tom Jones*, at the Opéra Comique. It was said at the time by someone speaking about the *Cercle*, where the society of that period is very well depicted, that Poinsinet must have listened behind the doors to know so well about its ins and outs. His end was very tragic. He was seized with a wish to travel, and began by visiting Spain, where he was drowned in crossing the Guadalquivir.

I must not forget to mention Davesne, a painter as well as a poet, but not by any means proficient in either art, whose very witty conversation made him always welcome at my father's house. I shall never forget, though I was so very young at the time, how cheerful those evenings used to be. I was made to leave the room before dessert, but from my room I could hear laughing, singing, and mirth, which to tell the truth I did not fully understand but which nevertheless made my holidays all the more delightful.

When I was eleven, I left the convent, after having been confirmed, and Davesne, who painted in oils, asked me to go to his house, so that he might teach me how to handle a palette. They were so poor that they were piteous to behold. One day they begged me to remain and dine with them, as I wished to finish a head I had commenced; and this meal was composed only of soup and roast potatoes.

It was a great pleasure to me not to leave my parents anymore. My brother, who was younger by two years than myself, was very handsome and wonderfully clever for his age; he progressed very quickly with his studies and was a great favorite with his masters, who used to send home most flattering accounts of his work. I was far from having his wit and brightness, and his pretty face, for at that time I was rather plain. I had an enormous forehead, my eyes were sunk deep in my head; my nose was the only good feature in my thin, pale face. I had grown so fast that I found it hard to stand upright, and I used to bend like a reed. All these imperfections were a great trial to my mother. I always knew she had a fancy for my brother rather than for myself, for she spoiled him, and forgave him very quickly when he was naughty while she was very severe with me. My father, on the contrary, made up for it by tending to me immensely. His tenderness endeared him very much to me, so that his memory seems always present with me, and I do not think I have forgotten a single word which he said before me. How many times have I remembered the following incident, in 1789, as a sort of prophecy! One day my father seemed so depressed and sad on leaving a dinner party where he had met Diderot, Helvétius, and d'Alembert that my mother asked him the reason. "All that I have heard, dear friend, shows me that the world will soon be turned upside down."

I will finish this long letter, my dearest, and embrace you with all my heart.

LETTER II

Up to the present time, dear friend, I have told you only of my joys; I must now tell you of the first affliction which I suffered and of my first real grief.

I had been at home for about one happy year when my father fell ill. He swallowed a fish bone which lodged in his throat, and several incisions had to be made in order to dislodge it. The wound became envenomed, and after two months of great suffering, my father's condition left no hope of recovery. My mother wept day and night, and I cannot describe to you my own grief. I was losing the best of fathers, my support and guide; he whose kindness encouraged my first attempts at painting.

When he felt himself dying, my father desired my brother and myself to approach. We drew near his bed, weeping bitterly. His face was cruelly altered; his eyes and face, usually so animated, were sunk and dimmed, for already the chill hand of death had laid itself upon him. We took his hand and covered it with kisses and tears. He made an effort to rise and gave us his benediction: "Be happy, my children," said he. An hour later our excellent father was no more.

My grief was so great that it was a long time before I could touch my pencils. Doyen came to see us sometimes, and as he had been my father's best friend, his visits were a great consolation. It was he who persuaded me to take up my beloved occupation again, and indeed I always found distraction and forgetfulness of my woes while I was painting. At this time I began painting from nature and from casts. I made several portraits in oils and pastels. I drew also landscapes and from casts with Mlle Boquet, whom I then knew. I spent the evening with her in the rue Saint-Denis, opposite the rue de la Truanderie, where her father kept a curiosity shop. It was a long way off, for we lived in the rue de Clêry, opposite the Hôtel de Lubert; consequently, my mother never allowed me to walk there alone.

At that time Mlle Boquet and myself used to draw a great deal with Briard, the painter, who lent us his designs and ancient busts to copy. Briard was not a very good painter, although he did some ceilings which were remarkable for their composition, but he was an excellent draftsman, which was the reason that several young artists came to take lessons from him. He lived at the Louvre. We had each our dinner brought us in a little basket by the servant, so that we might draw for a longer time.

Mlle Boquet was then fifteen years old, and I was fourteen. We were rival beauties, for I have forgotten to tell you, dear friend, that a complete metamorphosis had taken place in me, and that I had become pretty. She had remarkable talent, and my progress in painting was so rapid that people had begun to talk about me in the world, which caused me to have the satisfaction of knowing Joseph Vernet. That celebrated artist encouraged me and gave the best advice. "My child," said he, "do not follow any particular school. Only consult the works of the great Italian and Flemish masters; but, above all, do as much as you can from nature. Nature is the best master. If you study it diligently, you will never get into any mannerisms." I have always followed his advice, for, properly speaking, I have never had a master. As for Joseph Vernet, he has proved the excellence of his method by his works, which have been, and will be always, justly admired.

I also made the acquaintance of the Abbé Arnauld, of the Académie française. He was a man of much imagination, passionately fond of literature and art, whose conversation enriched my ideas. He spoke most enthusiastically about painting and music, and was an ardent partisan of Gluck. Later on he brought that great musician to my house, for I loved music also.

My mother was very proud of my looks and figure, for I had become plump again, which gave me the freshness of youth. On Sundays she used to walk with me in the Tuileries. She was still very beautiful herself at that time, and it is so long ago now that I do not mind telling you that we were followed about in such a manner that I was much more embarrassed than flattered by the attention we excited. My mother, seeing me always so depressed at the cruel loss I had had, thought the best thing to distract my mind was to take me to see paintings. We visited the Palais du Luxembourg, when the gallery was filled with the masterpieces of Rubens, and many other rooms crowded with the works of great masters. Now, one can see there the paintings of modern French artists; I am the only one who has none in that collection. These paintings have been since transported to the Musée du Louvre, and those of Rubens lose much from not being seen in the place they were painted. Well or badly hung pictures are like pieces of music well or badly played. We went also to see some good private collections. Randon de Boisset possessed a gallery of Flemish and French pictures. The Duc de Praslin and the Marquis de Lévis had rich collections from every school. M. Harens Le Preste had a beautiful one of Italian masters, but none could be compared with that of the Palais-Royal, which had been formed by the Regent, and which contained so many *chefs-d'œuvres* by great Italian masters. It was sold during the Revolution. An Englishman, Lord Stafford, bought most of the paintings.

From the time I entered one of these rich galleries, I could only be compared to a bee picking up knowledge and ideas for my art, and becoming quite intoxicated in the contemplation of great masters. I copied several paintings by Rubens, some by Rembrandt and Van Dyck, and several heads of young girls by Greuze, because these last thoroughly explained the semitones which are found in delicate carnations; Van Dyck explains them also, but much more delicately.

I owe to these studies the important knowledge of the gradations of light on the most projecting portions of the head, gradations which I admire so much in Raphael, who combines, indeed, every perfection. And, indeed, it is only in Rome, and under the beautiful Italian sky, that Raphael can justly be appreciated. When, later on, I was enabled to behold those of his masterpieces which have never left their country, I found Raphael to be above his immense reputation.

My father left no fortune; I earned a good deal of money already, having several portraits to take; but that did not suffice for the household expenses, seeing that I had also to pay for my brother's schooling, his clothes, and books. My mother was, therefore, compelled to remarry. She espoused a rich jeweler, whom we had never suspected of being avaricious, and yet who became immediately after his marriage so mean that he refused us the bare necessities of life, although I was good enough to give him all that I earned. Joseph Vernet was furious; he continually advised me to pay him a pension and keep the overplus for myself, but I did not do so. I was afraid lest with such a miser my mother would suffer. I hated this man all the more because he had appropriated my father's wardrobe and wore his clothes, just as they were, without any alterations. You can easily understand, dear friend, what a sad impression they made on me!

I had, as I have already told you, several portraits on hand, and already my youthful reputation attracted to me several foreigners. Many great Russian personages came to visit me, among others the celebrated Count Orlov, one of the assassins of Peter III. He was a colossal man, and I remember he wore a remarkably large diamond ring upon his finger. I painted almost immediately afterward the portrait of Count Shuvalov, Grand Chamberlain. He was then, I believe, about sixty, and had been the lover of the Empress Elizabeth II of Russia. He combined perfect politeness with charming manners, and, as he was a most agreeable man, he was sought by the best society.

I received at the same time the visit of Mme Geoffrin, whose *salon* made her so celebrated. Mme Geoffrin entertained at her house all the most distinguished literary and artistic men, foreigners, and courtiers. Without birth, talents, or any fortune to speak of, she created for herself in Paris a position unique in its way, and which no woman today would be able to accomplish. Having heard me spoken about, she came to see me one morning and made very flattering remarks on my person and talent. Although she was not very old then, I should have thought her at least a hundred, for not only did she stoop a great deal but her costume aged her immensely. She wore an iron-gray dress, with a large flapped cap, covered with a black hood tied under her chin. At her age, women nowadays, on the contrary, contrive to make themselves look younger by the care they take about their dress.

Soon after my mother's marriage, we lodged with my stepfather, in the rue Saint-Honoré, opposite the terrace of the Palais-Royal, onto which my windows looked. I often saw the Duchesse de Chartres walking in the gardens with her ladies, and I noticed that she looked at me with much interest and kindliness. I had just finished the portrait of my mother, which was much spoken of at the time. The duchess sent for me to paint hers at the palace. She communicated to those about her her great sympathy for my youthful talent, so that it was not long before I received the visit of the noble and beautiful Comtesse de Brionne and her daughter, the Princesse de Lorraine, who was extremely pretty, and after that of all the great ladies of the court and the faubourg Saint-Germain.

Since I have already told you, dear friend, how much attention I excited at promenades and other sights, so much so that I often had crowds around me, you can easily understand that several admirers of my countenance made me paint theirs also, in the hope of pleasing me, but I was so absorbed in my art that nothing had the power of distracting my thoughts. Besides, the moral and religious precepts inculcated by my mother protected me from the seductions with which I was surrounded. Fortunately for me, I had never read a single novel. The first I read (it was *Clarissa Harlowe*, which interested me extremely) was not till after my marriage; up to that time I read only religious books, *The Lives of the Holy Fathers*, among others, for everything is contained therein, and a few class books belonging to my brother.

But to return to these admirers. As soon as I discovered that they wanted to gaze at me with *les yeux tendres*, I painted them with the eyes averted, which prevented them from regarding the painter. And then, at the least movement round of their eyes, I said, "I am just at the eyes," which was annoying for them, as you can suppose. My mother, who never left me, and whom I had taken into my confidence, used to be much entertained.

On *fête* days and Sundays, after having heard Mass, my mother and stepfather used to take me out into the Palais-Royal. At that time the garden was much larger and more beautiful than it is now—hemmed in by houses. On the left there was a broad and very long alley, shaded by great trees, which formed a kind of arch, impenetrable to the sun. It was there that the beauty and fashion of Paris used to promenade. The opera was then close by; it was in the Palais-Royal. In summer it was over at half past eight, and all the most elegant women left even before it was over and adjourned to the garden instead. It was then the fashion for women to carry enormous bouquets, the odor of which, added to that of the strongly scented powder used in the hair, made the air seem quite embalmed. Long after, but before the Revolution, I have seen these reunions prolonged till two in the morning, with open-air music by moonlight. Many artists and amateurs sang there, including Garat and Alsevedo. It was crowded with people, and the famous Saint-Georges often played his violin.

It was there that I saw for the first time the elegant and pretty Mlle Duthé, who used to walk about with other women of light character; for in those days no gentlemen were ever seen with such people; if they joined them at the play, it was always in covered boxes. You have no idea, dear friend, what bad women were like in those days. Mlle Duthé, for instance, expended millions; now that trade is nowhere, few would ruin themselves for such women.

We never walked in that long alley of the Palais-Royal, Mlle Boquet and myself, without attracting great attention. We were then about sixteen and seventeen, and Mlle Boquet was very beautiful. In those days beauty was really an advantage. Mlle Boquet was remarkably talented, but she gave up painting soon after her marriage with M. Filleul, at which time the Queen appointed her keeper of the Château de la Muette. I wish I could tell you about this charming woman without recalling her tragic fate. Alas! I remember at the time I was leaving France to flee from the horrors which I foresaw, Mme Filleul said, "You are wrong to leave. I shall remain, for I believe in the happiness which this revolution will bring us." And that revolution led her to the scaffold! She had not left the Château de la Muette when those days, rightly called the Days of Terror, came upon France. Mme Chalgrin, daughter of Joseph Vernet and an intimate friend of Mme Filleul, was celebrating in the château her daughter's marriage, without any display as you can suppose. Nevertheless, the revolutionists came and arrested Mme Filleul and Mme Chalgrin, who, they said, had "burned the candles of the nation," and both were guillotined a few days afterward.

I will now finish this sad letter.

LETTER III

I will now again continue, dear friend, the thread of my narrative in what I call old Paris, the Paris of my youth, for this city has changed since then in every way. One of the most frequented promenades was the boulevard du Temple. Every day, but especially on Thursdays, hundreds of carriages passed to and fro, or were drawn up alongside alleys where are now cafés and shops. The young horsemen used to caracole around them as at Longchamps, for Longchamps existed even then. It was a brilliant scene, crowded with people admiring and criticizing the well-dressed women and beautiful equipages. One side of the boulevard, where the Café Turc now stands, presented a sight which has often made me laugh heartily. It was a long line of old fish-wives, sitting gravely on chairs with their cheeks so covered with rouge that they looked like dolls. As at that time only women of high rank could use rouge, these ladies considered they also were privileged to do the same to their heart's content. One of our friends who was acquainted with several of them told us that they played lotto from morning till evening when indoors, and that one day as he was returning from Versailles, one of them asked him for news. He replied that he had just been informed that M. de la Pérouse was about to sail round the world. "Really!" exclaimed the mistress of the house. "That man must have very little to do!"

The Coliseum was a promenade much in vogue; it

was placed in one of the great squares of the Champs-Élysées, in an immense rotunda. In the center was a lake, filled with limpid water, on which were held aquatic sports. You walked all round in broad pathways, sanded over and lined with seats. When it was dark everyone left the garden and adjourned to an immense salon, where you heard every evening excellent music with a good orchestra. Mlle Lemaure, very celebrated at that time, sang very often there, as well as many other celebrated singers. The broad flight of steps which led to this concert room was the rendezvous of all the young Parisian dandies, who, placing themselves beneath the illuminated doorways, never allowed a woman to pass without some epigram. One evening as I was descending the steps with my mother, the Duc de Chartres (afterward Philippe Egalité) was standing by, arm in arm with the Marquis de Genlis, the companion of his orgies, and the poor women who passed by did not escape from their most shameful sarcasms. "Ah! as for this one," said the duke in a loud voice, pointing to me, "there is nothing to be said!" This speech, which several others heard as well as myself, gave me so much satisfaction that even now I recall it with a feeling of pleasure.

About the same time there existed on the boulevard du Temple a place called the summer Vauxhall, of which the garden was composed of only a blank space destined for walking, and around which were covered benches for people to sit. My wretched stepfather, worried no doubt by the admiration received by my mother when in public, and, if I dare say so, from that which I created also, forbade our taking any promenades and told us one day he was going to take a country house. At these words my heart beat with joy, for I was passionately fond of the country. I wished to go there all the more because I slept nearly at the foot of my mother's bed, in a dark corner which the daylight never reached, so that in the morning, no matter what the weather was like, my first care was to open the window and breathe, so much did I need fresh air.

My stepfather hired a little bit of a house at Chaillot, and we slept there on Saturdays and returned to Paris on Monday morning. Heavens! What a place! Imagine a very tiny garden; no trees and no shade, except in a little arbor where my father had planted beans and runners which never grew. And we had not even the whole of this charming garden; it was divided into four parts by little sticks, and the three others were let to shop boys who used to spend their Sundays firing at the birds. This perpetual noise made me feel desperate; besides I was dreadfully afraid of being killed by these novices, they fired so badly. I could not understand why such a stupid unpicturesque place as this should be called the country; I was so bored there that it makes me yawn to write about it.

At last my guardian angel sent to my deliverance a friend of my mother's, Mme Suzanne, who came with her husband to dine at Chaillot. Both took pity on me and made me take some delightful excursions. We went first to Marly-le-Roi, where for the first time I saw an enchanting abode. On each side of the château, which was superb, were six pavilions, joined to each other by bowers of jasmine and honeysuckle. Cascades came rushing down a hill at the back of the château and formed a lake on which were stately swans. These beautiful trees, green bowers, basins, and fountains, one of which rose to such a height that it was lost to sight, were all grand and regal, for all bespoke Louis XIV. The sight of this exquisite place made such an impression on me that after my marriage I often returned to Marly.

It was there that I met one morning Queen Marie Antoinette, who was walking in the park with several of her court ladies. All were in white dresses and were so young and pretty that they looked like apparitions. I was with my mother, and we were retreating from them when the Queen had the goodness to stop and desired me to continue my promenade wherever I pleased. Alas! when I returned to France in 1802, I hastened to revisit my noble smiling Marly. The palace, trees, cascades, all had disappeared; I only found one stone left which seemed to mark the center of the salon.

I found it very hard to leave these lovely gardens and go back to gloomy Chaillot. At length, winter obliged us to return for good to Paris, where I passed the time very agreeably when my work allowed it. From the age of sixteen I had mixed in the best society, and knew all our first artists, so that I received invitations from all quarters. I remember very well dining the first time in Paris with Le Moyne, the sculptor, then very renowned. He was a man of great simplicity; but he had the good taste to bring together at his house a number of celebrated and distinguished characters. It was there I met the famous Lekain, whose fierce sullen looks frightened me; and Mme de Bonneuil, the prettiest woman in Paris, mother of Mme Regnault Saint Jean d'Angély; she was then as fresh as a rose. It was at Le Moyne's that I knew Gerbier, the lawyer; his daughter Mme de Boissy was very beautiful and was one of the first women whose portrait I took. Grétry and La Tour, two famous pastel painters, often assisted at these dinners; we laughed and amused ourselves well. It was the custom then to sing at dessert: Mme de Bonneuil, who had a charming voice, sang with her husband some of Grétry's duets; then came the turn of all the young girls, who were much tortured by this fashion, for they turned pale and trembled and often sang false in consequence. Notwithstanding, the dinner ended pleasantly, and we always left with regret, far from asking for our carriages in rising from the table, as is done nowadays.

I cannot speak much of the great dinners though, except by hearsay, seeing that shortly after the time of which I write, I ceased to dine in Paris at all. The daylight was really too precious for me to give its hours to society, and an accident which happened to me determined me to go out only in the evening. I had accepted a dinner with the Princesse de Rohan Rochefort; I was dressed and ready to step into a carriage when I thought I would go see a portrait which I had begun that morning. I wore a white satin dress which I had put on for the first time, and I sat down on a chair which was opposite to my easel without noticing that my palette was placed upon it; you may judge that I made my dress in such a mess that I was obliged to remain at home, and from that day I formed a resolution only to accept suppers.

The dinners of the Princesse de Rohan Rochefort were charming. The nucleus of her society was composed of the beautiful Comtesse de Brionne and her daughter, the Princesse de Lorraine, the Duc de Choiseul, Cardinal de Rohan, and M. de Rulhière, the author of the "Disputes"; but the most agreeable of all the guests was without contradiction the Duc de Lauzun; none other possessed such wit and humor. Often the evening was spent in music, and I sometimes sang and accompanied myself on the guitar. We had supper at half past ten and were never more than ten or twelve at table. It was a race for who could be most gay and witty. I only listened, and though too young to fully appreciate the charm of these conversations, they disgusted me with many others.

I have often told you, dear friend, that my life as a young girl was unlike that of most people. Not only did my talent, small as it appeared to me in contrast to the great masters, make me sought out and welcomed in every *salon*, but I received besides some marks of public sympathy, from which I frankly avow I derived much satisfaction. For instance, I had made from the engravings of the time the portraits of Cardinal Fleury and of La Bruyère. I presented them to the Académie française, which, through the medium of d'Alembert, its secretary, sent me the following letter which I copy here and which I have carefully preserved.

Mademoiselle,

The Académie française has received with much pleasure the charming letter which you have written to them, and the fine portraits of Fleury and of La Bruyère which you had the kindness to send to be placed in the Assembly Hall, where they have long desired to see them. These two portraits, in recalling two men whose names are cherished by them, will also bring back, mademoiselle, the remembrance of what they owe to you, of what they are proud to owe. Moreover, to their eyes these portraits will be a lasting memorial of your rare talents, which were known to them by public report, and which are heightened still more by your wit, grace, and great modesty.

The Company, wishing to show some token of gratitude in return for your kindness, in the manner most agreeable to yourself, pray you, mademoiselle, to be good enough to accept your free entry to all their public assemblies. That is what they decided yesterday in the assembly by unanimous deliberation, which was at once inscribed in the Registers, and with which I was charged to make you acquainted, in adding their sincere thanks. This commission pleases me all the more, because it gives me an opportunity of showing you, mademoiselle, the feelings of sincere esteem with which I have long been imbued for your talents and person, and which I share with all men of taste and honor.

I have the honor to be, mademoiselle, your very humble and obedient servant,

D'Alembert

Paris, August 10, 1775

The presentation of these two portraits to the Académie procured for me, shortly after, a visit from d'Alembert. He remained for some time and explored my studio, making several flattering speeches all the while. I have never forgotten that, after he had left, a great lady who happened to be there at the time, asked me if I had done those portraits of La Bruyère and of Fleury from life. "I am rather too young for that," I replied, laughing, but very glad, for the lady's sake, that the academician had left.

Adieu, dear friend!

LETTER IV

Dear friend, my stepfather having retired from business, we went to lodge in the Hôtel de Lubert, rue de Cléry. M. Le Brun had just bought this house, and as soon as we were settled, I went to see the splendid paintings of all schools with which his rooms were filled. I was delighted to be in the vicinity of so many masterpieces. M. Le Brun very kindly permitted me to copy and lent me for that purpose some very valuable and lovely paintings. I owed, therefore, my best lessons to him; and at the end of six months he made me an offer of marriage. I was not at all anxious to marry him, although he was well made and had a pleasant face. I was then twenty; I had no anxieties for my future, as I earned a good deal of money, so that I did not feel any desire to be married. But my mother, who fancied M. Le Brun was very rich, never ceased to urge me not to refuse such an advantageous *parti*. I at length consented to this marriage, as much from the longing to escape living with my stepfather, whose temper grew worse with every day he was inactive, as from anything else. So little was I inclined to renounce my liberty that in going to church I said to myself, "Shall I say yes? Shall I say no?" Alas! I said yes, and I exchanged my old troubles for other troubles. It was not because M. Le Brun was a bad man; his disposition was a great mixture of sweetness and vivacity; he was good-tempered with all—in a word, he was very amiable; but his headstrong passion for low women, added to a love of gambling, brought about the loss of his fortune and mine, which he entirely disposed of in such a complete manner that when I left France in 1789 I did not possess twenty francs, though I had then earned over a million. He had dissipated it completely.

My marriage was kept secret for some time. M. Le Brun begged me not to declare it publicly, as he ought to have espoused the daughter of a Dutchman, with whom he transacted a good deal of business concerning his paintings, and he wished it kept secret till his business was concluded. I consented willingly, for I regretted quitting my maiden name, under which I was very well known already; but this secrecy which did not last long had, nevertheless, rather a bad influence on my future. Several people who only thought I was intending to marry M. Le Brun came to see me to try to dissuade me from doing such a foolish thing. Now it was Aubert, court jeweler, who said, with an air of friendliness and truth, "You would do better to fasten a stone round your neck and throw yourself into the river than to marry Le Brun." Then it was the Duchesse d'Arenberg, accompanied by Mme de Canillac and Mme de Souza, wife of the Portuguese ambassador, all three so young and pretty, who brought me their tardy advice, when I had been already married a fortnight. "For heaven's sake!" said the duchess, "don't marry Monsieur Le Brun; you will be very unhappy." Then she related several things which I luckily did not quite believe, although they have since been confirmed; but my mother, who was there, could hardly restrain her tears. At length the declaration of my marriage put an end to these gloomy forebodings, which, thanks to my beloved painting, had not depressed me much. I could not paint all the portraits which were demanded of me on every side, and although M. Le Brun took upon himself to appropriate the payments, he did not hesitate to make me take pupils in order to augment our income. I consented to what he wished without reflecting on it, and soon there appeared several young ladies, to whom I had to give instructions as to how to make eyes and noses, which I was always compelled to retouch, and thereby lose much of my time at my own work, a very vexatious proceeding.

Among my pupils was a Mlle Emilie Le Roux de la Ville, who afterward married M. Benoist, Director of the Public Welfare, and for whom Demoustier wrote *Letters on Mythology*. She drew heads in chalk, and showed much talent, which gained for her a just reputation afterward. Mlle Emilie was the youngest of my pupils. They were mostly older than myself, which detracted from the respect due to the head schoolmistress. I had arranged a studio for these demoiselles in a large attic, with large beams running across it. One morning I went upstairs and found my pupils had fastened a rope round one of these beams and were busy swinging, as well as they could manage it. I put on a dignified air, grumbled, and made a long speech on wasting time; after which I tried the swing and had as much fun over it as the others. You can imagine that, with such lively ways, it was difficult for me to impress them much, and this circumstance, added to the bother of returning to the A, B, C of my art in correcting their studies, caused me to renounce having pupils at all.

The necessity of leaving my beloved brushes for a few hours conduced still more, I believe, to my fondness for my work. I never left my painting till it was quite dark, and the number of portraits I finished at that time was simply prodigious. As I had a great dislike to the costume worn by women in those days, I endeavored to render it more picturesque and felt enchanted when I obtained leave to drape my models as I pleased. Shawls were not worn then, but I arranged large scarfs by twining them lightly round the body and arms, seeking by that means to imitate the draperies of Raphael and Domenichino, which, perhaps, you have noticed in my Russian pictures, especially in the one of my daughter playing the guitar. Another of my prejudices was powder. I persuaded the lovely Duchesse de Gramont Caderousse not to wear any when she was painted. Her hair was as black as night, and I parted it in front and arranged it in careless locks. After my *séance*, which finished at dinnertime, the duchess went to the theater without altering her headdress. Such a pretty woman setting the fashion caused it soon to become popular; which reminds me that in 1786, while painting the Queen, I implored her not to wear powder and to divide her hair in front. "I shall be the last to follow that fashion," said the Queen, laughing. "I do not wish it to be said that I invented it, in order to hide my high forehead."

I sought as much as I possibly could to give to the ladies I painted the expression of their countenances. Those that had none in particular I painted with pensive looks, leaning nonchalantly against some object. I believe that they were well satisfied, for I could not work fast enough to satisfy the demand. It was a scramble to be placed on my list. In a word, I was the fashion. Everything conspired to keep me there. You may judge as much from the following scene which has always left a flattering impression on my mind: Shortly after my marriage, I attended a *séance* of the Académie française; La Harpe was reading his discourse on female talent, and when he came to these verses, where the praise is so exaggerated, and which I heard for the first time—"Le Brun de la beauté le peintre et le modèle, / Moderne Rosalba, mais plus brillant qu'elle, / Joint la voix de Favart au sourir de Venus, etc." (Le Brun, the painter and model of beauty, a modern Rosalba, but more brilliant than she, unites the voice of Favart with the smile of Venus)—the author of *Warwick* looked at me, and immediately the whole assembly, without excepting the Duchesse de Chartres and the King of Sweden, who were present, arose, turned toward me, and gave me such a transport of applause that I felt quite overcome.

These personal triumphs of which I have informed you, dear friend, because you desired me to tell you everything, are far from being compared with the joy I felt when, after two years of marriage, I hoped to become a mother. But here you will see how my extreme love for my art rendered me careless as to the small details of life, for, happy as I felt, I let the time pass by without preparing anything for myself. The day my daughter was born I never quitted my studio and worked at my *Venus Binding the Wings of Cupid* in the intervals between labor pains.

Mme de Verdun, my oldest friend, came to see me in the morning and asked me if I was provided with all that was necessary, as she knew how stubborn I was. I answered her, with much surprise, that I did not know what was necessary. "Just like you!" she answered. "You are a regular tomboy. I am certain you will have your child tonight." "No! no!" said I. "I have a sitting tomorrow. It cannot be today." Without replying, Mme de Verdun left me a short time to send for a doctor, who arrived soon after. I sent him away, but he remained, unknown to me, till the evening, and at ten o'clock my daughter was born.

During the previous months I had painted the Duchesse de Mazarin, who was no longer young but still retained the remains of great beauty; my daughter had her eyes, and was very like her. This Duchesse de Mazarin was said to have been endowed at her birth by three fairies; one with Riches, one with Beauty, and one with Ill Luck. It is very true that the poor woman could not undertake a single thing, even a *fête*, without some accident happening. Many are the stories told of various disasters which befell her. Here is one which is not so well known: One evening she gave a supper party to sixty people and thought she would have an enormous pie made, in which about a hundred little live birds were imprisoned. On a sign from the duchess, the pie was opened, and there burst forth all these terrified creatures, who flew into the faces and hair of the ladies present. You can imagine the uproar and screams. They could not get rid of these unfortunate birds and at last were forced to leave the table, grumbling at such a foolish joke. The Duchesse de Mazarin having become excessively stout, it took a long time to lace her stays. Someone paid her a visit one day while she was being laced up, and one of her waiting maids ran to the door, saying, "Don't come in till we have arranged the flesh." I remember that this great size excited much admiration from the Turkish ambassadors. When they were asked at the Opéra which woman pleased them best of all they had seen, they replied immediately the Duchesse de Mazarin.

Since I am writing about ambassadors, I will not omit to tell you how I painted two diplomats in my life who, though copper-colored, had, nonetheless, splendid heads. In 1788, some ambassadors were sent to Paris by the Sultan Tippu Saib. I saw these Indians at the Opéra, and they appeared to me to be so remarkably picturesque that I wished to paint their portraits. Having made their interpreter acquainted with my desire, I was informed they would never consent to be portrayed unless the demand came from the King. Therefore I obtained this favor of His Majesty. I went to the hotel which they inhabited; for they wished to be painted there, on large canvas and in colors. When I arrived in their salon, one of them arose, brought some rosewater and threw it over my hands, and then the grandest one gave me a sitting. I took him standing, holding his poignard. The draperies, hands, all were taken from life. He stood with such satisfaction and pleasure! I let the painting dry in another room, and I commenced the portrait of the old ambassador, whom I represented seated, with his son near him. Both were dressed in white muslin worked with gold flowers, and these robes, which are like tunics with large turned-back sleeves, were fastened with rich girdles. I finished the paintings on the spot, with the exception of some portions of the dress.

Mme de Bonneuil, to whom I had spoken about my sittings, had a strong desire to see these ambassadors. They invited us both to dinner, and we accepted, out of sheer curiosity. On entering the room, we were rather surprised to find the dinner served on the ground, which obliged us to sit, or rather lie down, round the table. They helped us with their hands from the different dishes. One contained a fricassee of sheep's trotters, with strongly spiced white sauce, and the other I know not what kind of stew. We made a sorry repast, as you can imagine.

When the portrait of Dervisch Khan was dry, I sent for it to be fetched away, but he had hidden it behind his bed and would not give it up, pretending that the painting wanted a soul. I could only obtain my portrait by a little ruse, and when the ambassador found it was missing, he became much enraged with his valet, whom he wanted to kill, and the interpreter had all the trouble in the world to make him understand that in Paris it was not the custom to kill valets. Finally, he had to tell him that the King of France desired the portrait. These two paintings were exhibited in the *Salon* of 1789. After the death of M. Le Brun, who had appropriated all my works, they were sold, and I know not who possesses them now.

Adieu, my dear, kind friend.

LETTER V

It was in the year 1779, my dear friend, that I took the Queen's likeness for the first time; she was then in all the brilliancy of her youth and beauty. Marie Antoinette was tall, admirably proportioned, plump, without being too much so; her arms were lovely, she had small and perfectly shaped hands and charming little feet. She walked better than any woman in France; holding her head very upright, with a majesty which denoted the Sovereign in the midst of her court, without this majestic bearing detracting in the least from the sweetness and grace of her whole aspect. In short, it is very difficult to give any idea to those who have not seen the Queen how very elegant and beautiful she was. Her features were not at all regular; she inherited the long narrow oval peculiar to the Austrian nation. Her eyes were not large and were almost blue in color; her expression was clear and very soft, her nose was thin and pretty, and her mouth was not large, although the lips were rather thick. The most remarkable thing about her face was the brilliancy of her complexion, I never saw anything like it, and "brilliant" is the only word to express what it was, for her skin was so transparent that it allowed of no shadow. I never could obtain the effect as I wished; paints failed to depict the freshness, the delicate tints of that charming face which I never beheld in any other woman. At first the imposing air of the Queen intimidated me extremely, but Her Majesty spoke to me with so much goodness that her kind manner soon dissipated this impression. It was then I made the portrait which represents her with a large panier, dressed in a satin robe, holding a rose. This picture was destined for her brother, the Emperor Joseph II, and the Queen ordered two copies of it: one for the empress of Russia, the other for her apartments at Versailles or Fontainebleau.

I made successfully, at various times, several other portraits of the Queen. In one portrait I only did her to the knees, with an orange-colored dress, seated before a table on which she was arranging flowers in a vase. As may be well believed, I preferred greatly to paint her without full toilette, and above all without a large panier. These portraits were given to her friends or ambassadors. Among them was one in which she was represented dressed in a white muslin dress, with the sleeves folded back, but carefully arranged all the same; when this was exhibited in the *Salon*, wicked people did not fail to say that the Queen had been painted in her chemise; for it was in 1786, and already calumnious reports began to be circulated about her. Nevertheless, this portrait had a great success. Toward the end of the exhibition, a little play was got up at the Vaudeville, which was called, I believe, *The Reunion of Art*. Brongniart, the architect, and his wife, who had been taken into the confidence of the author, engaged a box the day of the first representation and took me to the play. Having no idea of the surprise being prepared for me, my feelings may be imagined when I beheld this painting arrive and saw the actress who acted the part copy me in a most wonderful manner painting the Queen's portrait. At the same time, everyone arose from the boxes and stalls and turned toward me with vehement applause. I do not believe it was possible for any human being to be more deeply touched and gratified than I was that evening.

The timidity which the first sight of the Queen inspired entirely ceased, owing to the gracious kindness she always showed me. As soon as Her Majesty heard I had a pretty voice, she rarely gave me a sitting without making me sing with her several of Grétry's duets, for she was very fond of music, although her voice was not always in tune. As for her demeanor, it would be difficult to describe its affability and charm. I do not believe that Queen Marie Antoinette ever allowed an occasion to pass by without saying an agreeable thing to those who had the honor of approaching her, and the kindness which she always showed me is one of my most delightful souvenirs.

One day it so happened that I failed to appear at the time appointed for my sitting, because, owing to my health being very delicate at the time, I was taken suddenly ill. I hastened the next day to Versailles to make my excuses. The Queen had not expected me, and was going out driving in her carriage, which was the first thing I perceived on entering the courtyard of the château. All the same I went up and spoke to the gentlemen-in-waiting. One of them, M. Campan, received me very stiffly and said angrily, in his stentorian voice: "It was yesterday, madame, that Her Majesty expected you, and, of course, she is going driving, and, of course, she will not give you a sitting." On my saying that I came merely to take Her Majesty's orders for another day, he went to find the Queen, who immediately sent for me into her cabinet. She was finishing her toilette and held a book from which she was teaching her daughter. My heart beat fast, for I felt nervous, knowing I had been in the wrong. The Queen turned and said kindly, "I waited for you all yesterday morning; what happened to you?" "Alas! madame," I replied, "I was so ill that I was unable to attend Your Majesty's commands. I come today to receive them and will leave directly." "No! no! Do not leave," she rejoined. "I will not let you have your journey for nothing." She countermanded her carriage and gave me a sitting. I recollect that in my anxiety to make amends for her goodness, I seized my box of colors with such haste that I upset them all; my brushes and paints fell on the parquet, and I stooped down to collect them. "Let them alone, let them alone," said the Queen. "You are not in a condition to stoop," and not heeding what I said, she bent down and picked everything up herself.

At the time of the last journey to Fontainebleau, as the court, according to custom, had to be in full dress, I went there to behold the sight. The Queen was very magnificent, covered with diamonds, and as there was a bright sun to light her up, she appeared really dazzling. Her head being so beautifully set on her shoulders gave her, when walking, such an imposing and majestic air that she might have been a goddess surrounded by her nymphs. During the first sitting I had with her, after her return from this journey, I mentioned what an impression the sight had had on me, and told the Queen how much the manner she had of holding her head added to the dignity of her carriage; she answered in a laughing way: "If I were not Queen they would say I looked insolent; is it not so?"

The Queen never neglected an opportunity of teaching her children these gracious and affable manners which endeared her to all who had to do with her. I have seen her making Madame, then six years old, dine with a little peasant girl whom she protected, serving her first, and saying to her daughter, "You must do her the honors."

The last sitting I had from Her Majesty was at the Trianon, where I painted her head for the large picture in which I represented her with her children. After having finished the Queen's head, as well as separate studies for the first Dauphin, Madame Royal, and the Duc de Normandie, I busied myself about my picture for I considered it of great importance, and I finished it, for the *Salon* of 1788. The frame having been taken there by itself was sufficient to cause numerous evil speeches. "Voilà la deficit," they said, and many other things were told to me, showing me that I should have some harsh criticisms. At last, I sent my painting, but I had not courage to follow it and know my fate, so much did I dread it would meet with a bad reception from the public. My fear was so great that it made me feverish; I shut myself in my room and was there praying to God for the success of *my* Royal Family, when my brother and crowd of friends came to tell me I had obtained universal approbation.

After the *Salon*, the King had the picture taken to Versailles. It was M. d'Angiviller, then Minister of Arts and Director of the Royal Establishment, who presented me to His Majesty. Louis XVI had the goodness to talk some time with me, and to say he was much pleased. Then he added, again looking at my work, "I do not understand much about painting, but you make me love it."

My picture was placed in one of the rooms of the Château of Versailles, and the Queen always passed it in going to and returning from Mass. After the death of the Dauphin, at the beginning of 1789, the sight of it recalled so vividly her sad loss that she could no longer traverse this room without weeping. She told M. d'Angiviller to have the painting removed; but with her habitual kindness had me at once informed of her reason for so doing. It is to this sensitiveness on the Queen's part that I owe the preservation of my work; for the bandits and fishwives, who came shortly after to seek their Majesties at Versailles, would have certainly pierced it through and through, as they did the Queen's bed.

I never had the good fortune to see Marie Antoinette again after the last court ball at Versailles; this ball was given in the theater, and the box where I was seated was near that of the Queen, so that I could hear what she said. I thought her very agitated, inviting some of the young men about the court, such as M. de Lameth, to dance with her (his family had been treated with much favor by the Queen), and others also, who all refused; so that several of the quadrilles and dances could not be arranged at all. The behavior of these gentlemen struck me as being most unbecoming; I do not know why, but their refusal seemed to me to be a kind of evil omen, a prelude to graver ills. The Revolution was very near; it broke out the next year.

With the exception of the Comte d'Artois, I painted all the royal family in succession; the children of France; Monsieur, brother of the King, afterward Louis XVIII; Madame, Mme la Comtesse d'Artois, and Mme Elizabeth. The features of the latter were not at all regular, but her face expressed a sweet disposition, and her complexion was wonderfully fresh; she possessed the charm of a pretty milkmaid. You must not forget, dear friend, that Mme Elizabeth was an angel of goodness. How often have I seen her succoring the poor and afflicted! Her heart was filled with kindness; indulgent, modest, sensible, and devoted. The Revolution showed how heroic she was. We saw her, that lovely princess, walk in front of the cannibals who came to assassinate the Queen, saying, "They will take me for her!"

The portrait I made of Monsieur gave me an opportunity of knowing a prince whose wit and culture one could praise without flattery; it was impossible not to be pleased with the conversational powers of Louis XVIII. He spoke on all subjects with taste and knowledge. Occasionally, though, he used to sing to me, during our sittings, to vary them no doubt, some songs which were not immoral exactly but so vulgar that I could not imagine how such rubbish ever reached the court. His voice was never in tune. "How do you think I sing, Madame Le Brun?" he asked one day. "Like a prince, monsieur," I replied.

The Marquis de Montesquiou, equerry to Monsieur, sent a handsome carriage and six horses to take me to Versailles and back with my mother, whom I begged to accompany me. All the way, people ran to their windows to see me pass, and took off their hats to me; I laughed at the homage and respect paid to the six horses and outrider; for back in Paris I drove about in flys, and no one thought of looking at me then.

Monsieur was then what is called a liberal, in the moderate sense of the word; he and his followers formed a distinct party from the King's. So that I was not at all surprised to see, during the Revolution, that the Marquis de Montesquiou was appointed General-in-Command of the Republican forces in Savoy. I then recalled the strange conversations he had held before me, not to mention the tales which he openly related against the Queen and those who loved her; as for Monsieur, the newspapers told us how he went to the National Assembly and said he did not come to sit there as a prince but as a citizen. I do not believe though that that declaration would have sufficed to save his head, and he did well to leave France shortly afterward.

At the same time I painted the Princesse de Lamballe. Without being pretty, she looked so at a little distance; she had small features, a brilliant complexion, splendid blond hair, and an elegant figure. The horrible fate of this unfortunate princess is well known, as well as the devotion to which she fell a victim, for in 1793 she was safe from all danger at Turin, when she returned to France on hearing of the danger the Queen was in.

There! I am a long way from 1779, dear friend; but I preferred relating to you in one letter the dealings I had as an artist with all these great people, of whom today none are left but the Comte d'Artois, Charles X, and the unfortunate daughter of Marie Antoinette.

LETTER VI

Dear friend, in 1782 M. Le Brun took me to Flanders, where he had some business to transact. There was then a sale at Brussels of the splendid collection of paintings of Prince Charles, and we went to see the exhibition. I met several of the court ladies there who greeted me most kindly, among them the Princesse d'Arenberg, whom I had seen in Paris; but the meeting which pleased me most was with the Prince de Ligne, whom I did not know before and who has left, I may say, a historical reputation behind him for wit and amiability. He invited us to see his gallery, where I admired several masterpieces, principally portraits by Van Dyck and heads by Rubens, for he had few Italian paintings. I remember his taking us to see his beautiful seat at Beœil; we ascended a belvedere, built on the top of a hill which commanded a view over all his property and the country round. The delicious air and lovely view were most enchanting; but everything was eclipsed in this charming place by the greeting and bearing of the master of the house, who for elegance of mind and manners has never had an equal.

We left Brussels for Holland and the North. Zaandam and Mars pleased me extremely; these two little towns are so clean and well kept that I envied the inhabitants. The streets were very narrow, and being bordered by canals, carriages were not used, but people went on horseback and employed little barques for the transport of merchandise. The houses, which were very low, had two doors; one for birth, and one for death, which was only used for coffins. The roofs of these houses were as shining as though they were made of steel. The women in this part of Holland are very pretty, but very shy; the sight of a stranger made them fly. They were like that in those days; I suppose though that having French people sojourning in their country has made them less timid since.

We finished by visiting Amsterdam, and there I saw at the Hotel de Ville the wonderful painting by Wanols, representing the burgomasters assembled. I do not believe there exists any painting more lifelike or finer of its kind; it is so true to nature. The burgomasters are dressed in black: their heads, hands, and draperies are wonderfully painted. The impression made on me by this painting is so vivid that I seem to see it even now.

We returned to Flanders to see the masterpieces of Rubens again. They were better placed then than they have been since in the museum at Paris, for their effect in the old Flemish churches was beautiful. Other paintings by the same master adorned the amateurs' gallery; at Antwerp I discovered in a private collection the famous "Straw Hat," which was recently sold to an Englishman for a considerable sum of money. This wonderful painting represents one of Rubens's wives; its principal effect consists in the different lights given by the sun, daylight and the sun's rays. Perhaps only a painter can judge of its merits and wonderful execution. I was enchanted with this picture, and when I returned to Brussels I made a portrait of myself and endeavored to obtain the same effect. I wore on my head a straw hat, a feather, and a garland of field flowers, and held in my hand a palette. When the portrait was exhibited in the *Salon*, I may say that it added a good deal to my previous reputation. The celebrated Müller engraved it; but the dark shadows of an engraving take away from the effect of such a painting.

Shortly after my return from Flanders in 1783, the portrait I have just told you about and several other of my works decided Joseph Vernet to propose me as a member of the Académie royale de peinture et de sculpture. M. Pierre, then chief painter to the King, was strongly opposed to it, as he did not, he said, wish women to be received; and yet Mme Vallayer-Coster, who painted flowers most beautifully, had already been received, and I believe Mme Vien also. However that may be, M. Pierre (a very second-rate artist, for he only saw in painting the art of handling the brush) was a clever man; and besides he was rich, which gave him the means of receiving artists, who in those days were less fortunate than they are now. His opposition might have been fatal to me, if in those times all the true amateurs had not been associates of the Académie, and had they not formed, in my favor, a cabal against that of M. Pierre. Finally I was admitted. M. Pierre then spread about a report that it was through an order from the court that I had been received. I really believe that the King and Queen had been good enough to wish me to enter the Académie, but that was all.

I gave for a presentation picture *Peace Bringing Back Abundance*, which is now in the Ministère de l'Intérieur. It ought to have been returned to me, as I no longer belong to the Académie. I continued painting very hard; I had often three sittings in one day, and those after dinner tired me so much that I became thinner and thinner, owing to no longer being able to digest well. My friends got the doctor to order me to sleep every day after my dinner. At first it was difficult to accustom myself to this habit, but as I remained in my room with the shutters closed, sleep at last overtook me, and I am sure it is to this prescription that I owe my life. You know, dear friend, how much importance I ascribe to keeping calm. Being forced to work so hard, added to the fatigue of my long voyages, rendered it positively necessary; the only objection I had to this siesta was that it deprived me of the pleasure of dining in town, and as I devoted the whole morning to painting, I never saw my friends until the evening. It is true that then I could do as I pleased, for I spent my evenings in the most delightful and brilliant society.

After my marriage, I still lived in the rue de Cléry, where M. Le Brun had a large suite of rooms, very richly furnished, in which he kept his paintings by the great masters. As for me, I was reduced to occupying a little anteroom and bedroom, which served me as a sitting room. This room was hung with the same material as my bed-curtains. The furniture was extremely simple, too much so, perhaps, which however did not prevent M. de Champcenetz writing (his mother-in-law was jealous of me) that "Madame Le Brun had splendid hangings to her rooms, that she lighted her fire with bank notes, and only burned aloe wood"; but I will not tell you now, dear friend, any more of the calumnies of which I have been the victim; we shall go back to them by and by. They are explained by my receiving every evening in these modest small apartments, which I have described, both courtiers and townsfolk; great ladies, noblemen, and men of mark in letters and art—all came to these rooms; it was who would be present at my receptions, and often the marshals of France had to sit on the floor—I remember the Maréchal de Noailles, who was very large and very old, had one night the greatest difficulty in getting up again.

I was far from imagining that all these great people came on my account; as so often happens where open house is kept, some came to meet their friends, and others, the greater number, to enjoy the best music which was to be had in Paris. The celebrated composers Grétry, Sacchini, and Martini often performed at my house portions of their works before the first representation. Our most constant singers were Garat, Alsevedo, Richer, Mme Todi, and my sister-in-law, who had a beautiful voice and could accompany anything by sight, which was very useful to us. I, too, sang occasionally, without much training it is true, for I had never the time for lessons, but my voice was agreeable; the amiable Grétry said I had most silvery tones. However we must put aside all pretensions as to singing when one mentions those I have just named, for Garat may be cited as one of the most extraordinarily talented men ever met with. Not only was there nothing too difficult for that flexible voice, but for expression he had no rival, none ever sang Gluck as well as he did. Mme Todi combined a superb voice with all the qualities of a great singer, and she sang serious and buffo parts equally well. For instrumental music I had Viotti, the violinist, whose touch was exquisitely soft and delicate, Jarnović, Mestrino, and Prince Henry of Prussia, an excellent amateur who brought his first violin. Sallantin played the hautboy, Hüllmandel and Cramer the piano. Mme de Montgeron came once soon after her marriage. Although she was very young then, she astonished everyone by her expression and execution.

The ladies who usually attended my concerts were the Marquise de Grollien, Mme de Verdun, the Marquise de Sabran, who afterward married the Chevalier de Boufflers, the Comtesse de Mailly (all four great friends of mine), the Comtesse de Ségur, the Marquise de Rougé, Mme de Pezay, her friend—I painted them together—and a host of other ladies whom I could not receive very often owing to the small space afforded by my rooms, and several distinguished foreigners. As for the men, it would take too long to name them, as I believe I entertained all of any note in Paris.

I selected the most amiable among these to invite to my supper parties, which were the most amusing in Paris, owing to the presence of the Abbé Delille, the poet Le Brun, the Chevalier de Boufflers, the Vicomte de Ségur, and many others, who were among my most favored guests. No one can imagine what society was like in France in those days when, business being over, twelve or fifteen people would visit at different friends' houses and there finish the evening. The mirth and laughter which presided at these entertainments gave them a charm which mere dinners can never have—a friendliness and sociability reigned among the guests, restraint was laid aside, and it was at the suppers that Parisian society showed its superiority over that of all Europe. At my house, for instance, people began to arrive at nine o'clock. Politics were never alluded to, but literature and the news of the day were the chief subjects of conversation. Sometimes we amused ourselves with acting charades, sometimes the Abbé Delille or Le Brun-Pindare would recite some of their verses. At ten we sat down to table; my supper was a most simple repast. It was always composed of a fowl, a fish, a dish of vegetables, and a salad; so that if I happened to have too many guests there was not always enough for all to eat. It was not of much consequence, we were gay, good-tempered, and the hours passed like minutes; toward midnight all took their departure.

Not only did I have suppers at my own residence, but I frequently supped in Paris. I enjoyed then taking some repose after my labors in the form of cheerful distractions. Occasionally it was a ball, a ball where people were not crushed as they are now; eight people were sufficient to form a quadrille, and the women who did not dance could at any rate watch the dancing, for the men stood upright behind them. Never having cared about dancing, I preferred the houses where music was the attraction. I often went to spend the evening with M. de Rivière, who was chargé d'affaires to the Court of Saxony, as he was distinguished both for his wit and moral qualities. His daughter, my sister-in-law, sang divinely and made a good amateur actress. The eldest son of M. de Rivière was charming in comic parts; I took the part of a soubrette in operas and comedies. Mme La Ruette, who had retired from the stage some years before, did not disdain joining our troupe. She acted in several operas with us, and her voice was still fresh and very lovely. My brother Vigée took the first parts very well; in fact all our actors were excellent, except Talma. You will laugh at this, but the fact is that Talma, who acted the lovers' parts, was awkward and embarrassed, and no one could have foreseen that he would become an inimitable actor. My surprise was great, I confess, when I beheld our *jeune premier* outdo Larive and even Lekain. But the time it took to work this metamorphosis, and all those of the same nature, proves to me that dramatic talent is one of the last to develop itself. If you take the trouble to look around, you will find that there never yet existed any actor who was great in his youth.

Ever your friend.

LETTER VII

Here, my dear friend, is an exact account of the most brilliant supper I ever gave. One evening I had invited twelve or fifteen friends to hear a reading of the poet Le Brun. While I was resting, before they arrived, my brother read me some pages of the *Travels of Anacharsis*. When he reached the part describing Greek dinners, and the different sauces and food they had, he said, "We ought to try some of those things tonight." I immediately spoke to my cook and told her what to do, and we decided she should make one sauce for the fowl and another for the eels. As I was expecting some very pretty women, I thought we might all dress up in Greek costumes so as to create a surprise for M. de Vaudreuil and M. Boutin, who we knew could not arrive before ten. My studio, full of the things with which I draped my models, provided me with several clothes, and the Comte de Parois, who lodged in my house, had a fine selection of Etruscan vases. He came to see me that day, as it happened; I informed him of my project, and he brought me a quantity of vases to choose from. I dusted them carefully and placed them on a mahogany table, laid without a cloth. I then placed a large screen behind the chairs, which I concealed by covering it here and there with a drapery, like that which is seen in some of Poussin's paintings. A hanging lamp threw a strong light on the table. At last everything was prepared, even my costumes; the first to arrive was a daughter of Joseph Vernet, the charming

Mme Chalgrin. Immediately I dressed her hair and draped her. Then came Mme de Verneuil, renowned for her beauty, and Mme Vigée, my sister-in-law, who without being pretty had the most lovely eyes. And there they were, all three metamorphosed into veritable Athenians. Le Brun-Pindare came in, we took off his powder and undid his side curls, and on his head I placed a wreath of laurel with which I had painted young Prince Henry Lubomirski. I had represented him kneeling before a laurel bush and plaiting a crown. This painting has always remained in the family; the King of Poland told me, when at St. Petersburg, that never would they consent to part with it at any price, even to him. The Comte de Parois had a large purple mantle in which I draped my poet, and in a twinkling there was Pindare transformed into Anacreon. Then came the Marquis de Cubières. While they went to his house for his guitar, which he had had mounted as a golden lyre, I costumed him also, as well as M. de Rivière (my sister-in-law's brother), Ginguené, and Chaudet, the famous sculptor.

It was getting late, I had not much time to think of myself; but as I always wore white tunic-shaped dresses, now called blouses, I only needed a veil and crown of flowers on my head. I took great pains with my daughter, a charming child, and Mlle de Bonneuil, now Mme Regnault d'Angély, who was very pretty. Both were most graceful to behold, bearing each an antique vase and waiting on us.

At half past nine the preparations were over, and as soon as we were seated the effect of this arrangement was so novel and picturesque that we kept rising in turns in order to look at those who were seated. At ten we heard the carriage of the Comte de Vaudreuil and M. Boutin, and when these two gentlemen entered the room, they found us singing the chorus from Gluck, the god of Paphos and Guido, with M. de Cubières accompanying us on his lyre. I never in my life saw two such astonished faces as those of M. de Vaudreuil and his companion. They were surprised and delighted, and could hardly tear themselves away from looking at us in order to sit down in the places reserved for them. Besides the two dishes I have mentioned, we had a cake made of honey and Corinthian grapes, and two plates of vegetables. We did indeed drink that evening a bottle of old Cyprian wine, which I had had given me, but that was our only excess. We sat a long time at table, and Le Brun recited several odes to us. We all spent a most enjoyable evening.

M. Boutin and M. de Vaudreuil were so enthusiastic about it that they spread it abroad the next day among their friends. Some court ladies asked me for a second representation of this amusement, but I refused for several reasons, and many of them were annoyed with me in consequence. Soon the rumor spread that this supper cost me twenty thousand francs. The King spoke angrily about it to the Marquis de Cubières, who luckily was able to tell him how much it had been exaggerated.

Nevertheless what was rumored at Versailles at twenty thousand francs spread to Rome at forty thousand; at Vienna, the Baronne de Stroganov informed me

I had spent sixty thousand on my supper, and at St. Petersburg, as you know, the sum remained at eighty thousand, whereas, to tell the truth, my Greek supper cost me only fifteen francs. The saddest part of all this was that these shameful stories were carried round Europe by my own compatriots, and this ridiculous calumny was not the only one with which my life was made unhappy; it is only too true that since I made my appearance in the world I have been a prey to malevolence and stupidity. One tale was that my works were not done by myself, that M. Ménageot painted my pictures and even my portraits, although so many people could naturally bear witness to the contrary. This absurd report did not cease till I had been received at the Académie royale de peinture. Then as I exhibited in the same *Salon* as the author of Meleager, the truth came out, for Ménageot, whose talent and counsels I fully appreciated, had a style of painting quite different from mine. His pictures are finely composed and in a good historical style. This artist excelled in his draperies, and his Leonardo da Vinci, dying in the arms of Francis I, is very remarkable, but not equal to the Meleager at the Gobelins.

Although I believe I was a most inoffensive person, I had enemies: not only among women, who disliked my not being as plain as they were, but some men could not forgive me for being the vogue, and for getting more money for my paintings than they did. The result was many gossiping stories, one of which distressed me very much. Shortly before the Revolution I made a portrait of

M. de Calonne and exhibited it at the *Salon* of 1785. I had painted this minister seated, a half-length picture, which caused Mlle Arnould to say, when she saw it, "Madame Le Brun has cut off his legs so that he may not run away." Unfortunately, this witty remark was not the only one to which my painting gave rise; the most dreadful calumnies were invented about the picture. Some asserted that the Controller-General had given me a number of those bonbons, called curlpapers, wrapped up in bank notes; others that I had received in a pasty a sum large enough to ruin the Exchequer. The truth was that M. de Calonne had sent me four thousand francs in a box valued at twenty louis; several people are still alive who were present when I received it and can certify to the truth of my statement. They were surprised at the smallness of the sum, for shortly before M. de Beaujon, whom I had painted in the same way, sent me eight thousand francs (three hundred and twenty pounds) and no one found the price exorbitant, even then. The stone once set rolling, there were no end of evil-disposed persons to keep it going. I was harassed with libels, accusing me of having a secret liaison with M. de Calonne. A man named Gorsas, whom I never knew or saw and who was a violent Jacobite, deluged me with wicked lies.

The misfortune was that M. Le Brun, who, against my wishes, had built a house in the rue Gros-Chenet, gave by this means a pretext for calumny. Certainly we had both earned sufficient money to allow of this expense; nevertheless, certain people asserted that M. de Calonne paid for the house. "You see," I frequently said to M. Le Brun, "what infamous stories they tell of me!" "Let them talk," he replied in just indignation. "When you die, I will erect a pyramid in my garden, and on it I will have engraved the list of your portraits; they will know then what a fortune you have made." But I must own that this honor consoled me very slightly for my present annoyance. This annoyance was all the more keen, as no one more than myself could possibly fear becoming the object of degrading thoughts. I was so indifferent on the subject of money that I scarcely knew its value; the Comtesse de la Guiche, who is still alive, could affirm that having come to arrange the price of her portrait which she wished me to make, told me that she could not afford to pay more than a thousand crowns; I replied that M. Le Brun would not allow me to take less than a hundred louis. This defect of calculation I found very disadvantageous to me during my last journey to London; I constantly forgot that guineas were worth more than a louis, and for my portraits (among others, that of Mme Canning in 1803) I made my account as though I was in Paris.

All those who surrounded me knew that M. Le Brun took possession of all the money I earned, telling me that he required it for his business; frequently I had only six francs in my purse. In 1788, when I made the portrait of the handsome Prince Lubomirski, then a youth, his aunt the Princesse Lubomirski sent me twelve thousand francs, and I begged M. Le Brun to let me have two louis; but he refused, pretending that he had need of the entire sum to pay a debt. Besides this, M. Le Brun frequently appropriated money that was paid, and neglected to tell me that I had been paid. Once in my life, in the month of September, 1789, I received the price of a portrait; it was that of the Bailly de Crussol, who sent me one hundred louis. Happily, my husband being absent, I was able to keep this sum, which a few days afterward, on the fifth of October, enabled me to journey to Rome.

My indifference to money was no doubt caused by the small need I had to be rich. I lived very quietly and spent little on my toilette; I was often reproached with negligence on this point, for I wore generally nothing but white dresses, either muslin or linen, and I never wore full dress except for my *séances* at Versailles. My head-dress cost me nothing, I arranged my hair myself, and generally twisted round my head a muslin kerchief, as can be seen in the portraits of myself which are in Florence, St. Petersburg, and at Paris at M. de Laborde's. In all my portraits I am painted thus, with one exception, which is at the Musée du Louvre, where I am attired as a Greek.

The most surprising part of this affair was that there had never been a shadow of truth in the calumny; I scarcely knew M. de Calonne. Once only in my life had I been in his house, on the occasion of his giving a grand *soirée* to Prince Henry of Prussia, and he had thought it proper to invite me. I recollect having finished his portrait in so much haste that I did not copy his hands, which I was always in the habit of doing from my models.

I should therefore never have imagined from what source these malignant stories could have arisen, had I not discovered afterward a most perfidious action worthy of the lower regions.

In fact, is there ever a great reputation made that does not excite envy? It is true that it draws to you all your most distinguished contemporaries, and this society is a great consolation. When I think of the many amiable, kind people whose acquaintance and friendship I owe to my art, I am happy that my name is known.

Adieu.

LETTER VIII

My greatest recreation was going to the theater, and I can assure you that at the time of which I write the actors were so admirable that they have never been excelled. I perfectly recollect having seen the celebrated Lekain act, though I was too young to appreciate his great talent. At the time when Lekain played his first parts, and even some years later, I saw Brizard and Mlle Dumesnil. Brizard took the parts of the "fathers," and nature seemed to have fitted him for this employment; his white hair, imposing stature, and his superb voice gave him the most noble and respectable appearance imaginable. He excelled most in *King Lear*, and in the *Œdipus* of Ducis. You would really have thought you saw these unfortunate princes, so grand was the aspect of the man who represented them.

Mlle Dumesnil, though small and very plain, excited the greatest enthusiasm in the tragic parts. Her talent, however, was uncertain; she fell sometimes into trivialities, but she had also sublime moments. In general, she expressed passion better than tenderness, unless it was maternal, for one of her best parts was Merope. It sometimes happened that Mlle Dumesnil, in playing a part of the piece, produced no effect on her audience; suddenly she would become animated, and then her manner, her voice, her look, all became so eminently tragic that she carried the whole house with her. I am told that before appearing on the stage, she always drank a bottle of wine, and had one in reserve behind the scenes.

One of the most remarkable actors at the Théâtre-Français in tragedy and high comedy was Monvel. Some physical disadvantages, and a weak voice, precluded him from taking a first place; but his spirit, his enthusiasm, and above all the correctness of his diction left nothing to be desired. On my return to Paris, he had quitted the role of *jeunes premiers* for that of *pères nobles*. I saw him play Augustus of Cinna and l'Abbé de l'Épée in an admirable manner; in this last piece he was so perfectly natural that once on leaving the scene he bowed to the actors of the piece; I rose and returned his bow, which greatly amused the friends I was with.

The most brilliant debut which I remember and have seen was that of Mlle Raucourt in the role of Dido. She was not more than eighteen or twenty years of age. The beauty of her face, figure, voice, and diction all promised a perfect actress; joined to all her other advantages, she had a remarkably modest manner and an unblemished reputation, which made her much sought after by all the great ladies of Paris. They gave her jewelry, costumes for the theater, and money for herself and father, whom she never left. She acted at the theater until her death, playing the parts of mothers and queens with infinite success.

Talma, our last great tragic actor, surpassed to my mind all the others. There was genius in his acting. One may also say that he revolutionized art: in the first place by his true and pure diction, and next in insisting on an innovation in the costumes, attiring himself as a Greek or Roman, as the case might be, to play Achilles or Brutus, for which I felt deeply obliged to him. Talma had a splendid head and the most expressive face, and no matter to what lengths the fire of his acting carried him, he was always dignified, which to me appears one of the first qualities in a tragic actor. His voice was sometimes a little hollow, and was most suitable to express rage or profound emotion; he shone most in the roles of Orestes and Manlius; but in all he was generally sublime. The last role which he created has never been played by anyone since. Talma was an excellent man, and one of the easiest to get on with that could be possibly met. He did not appear to care much about shining in society; to draw him out it was necessary that the conversation should touch on anything which interested his heart and mind; then he became very interesting to listen to, especially when he conversed on his art.

Comedy at this time was perhaps even richer in talent than tragedy. I often had the pleasure of seeing Préville act. It was delightful and inimitable! His style was so natural, sparkling, and gay! No matter what he played, whether Crispin, Sosie, Figaro, you would not have recognized him to be the same man, he had so many different ways of acting comic parts; he was so true to nature that all who have tried to imitate him have only shown how indifferent they were.

Dugazon, his successor in comic parts, would have made an excellent comedian had he not been possessed with the desire of always making the public laugh, which often became quite a farce. He played certain parts perfectly; that of a valet for instance. His conduct during the Revolution was atrocious: he was one of those who brought back the King from Varennes; an eyewitness told me he saw him at the door of the carriage, his gun on his shoulder. Remember that this man had been most kindly treated by the court, and principally so by the Comte d'Artois.

At the time that all these great actors of whom I am telling you began to grow old, there arose among them a young genius who is now the ornament of the French stage. Mlle Mars then acted in the more simple parts most inimitably; she excelled as Victorine in the *Philosophe sans le savoir*, and in twenty parts in which she has never been equaled, she was so thoroughly natural and true. Fortunately that face, figure, and voice are so well preserved that Mlle Mars has no age and will, I am sure, never be old; every evening the delight of the public shows they are of my opinion.

One of the most beloved actors was Cailleau. He left the stage when I was still very young, but I saw him act twice in *Annette and Lubin*. When the Revolution broke out he was much suspected, as he had received many kindnesses from the Comte d'Artois. I was told, but I will not believe, that he proved ungrateful and played the part of Jacobin. If it is true, I am convinced that the fear of his wife turned his head. I have good reasons for believing that she was a Republican; in 1791 I received in Rome a letter from her imploring me to return to France, saying that we should be all equal, and it would be a *golden age*. Happily I did not believe her, for what an age of gold succeeded! Shortly after getting this letter, I heard Mme Cailleau had thrown herself out of a window in a fit of despair.

And now I come to her whose dramatic career I have followed from beginning to end, to the most perfect actress ever possessed by the Opéra Comique, to Mme Dugazon. Noble, naive, graceful, and piquant, she had twenty faces, and always suited her accent to the person she represented at the time. Mme Dugazon was a Royalist to the core, and gave strong proof of that to the public at an advanced period of the Revolution. One evening as she was acting the soubrette in the *Evénements Imprévus*, the Queen attended the representation, and in a duet where the valet begins by saying, "I love my master tenderly," Mme Dugazon, who had to reply, "Ah! how I love my mistress," turned toward the Queen's box, put her hand on her heart, and sang her reply in a feeling voice, bowing to the Queen. I have been told that later on the public—and what a public!—wished to be revenged on her for this noble act, and endeavored to make her sing some horrible song, which they delighted in, on the stage; Mme Dugazon would not yield, but left the theater.

The length of this letter will show you, dear friend, how much I liked acting. Adieu.

To my great regret, I was unable to remain long in the country; but I often spent two or three days there at a time, and I had invitations to all the most beautiful places round Paris. I saw the Chantilly *fêtes*, organized by the Prince de Condé, who afterward returned to France with Louis XVIII, and who knew so well how to do the honors of those entertainments. You know the beautiful château at Chantilly; the long gallery was adorned with armor of different epochs, some of it so heavy and large that it might have done for giants. At the end of the gallery was the cast of Henry IV, taken from his face after his death, to which still adhered some of the hair belonging to the eyebrows of the great king. I do not know what has become of this mask, which has been often reproduced in plaster; the armory was pillaged in the Revolution, and a good deal of it found its way into museums.

In 1782, I stayed some time at Raincy. The Duc d'Orléans, father of Philippe Egalité, who then lived there, invited me to take his portrait and that of Mme de Montesson. With the exception of the large hunts which I enjoyed watching, I felt rather bored at Raincy; my sittings over, I had no congenial society except that of Mme Berthollet, a very pleasant woman, who played well on the harp. While mentioning this visit, I cannot recall now without laughing a peculiarity of those days which at the time shocked me; while Mme de Montesson gave me a sitting, the old Princesse de Conti came one day to visit her, and this princess, in speaking to me, called me always "Miss." I was then expecting the birth of my daughter, which rendered this term still more curious. It is true that formerly all the great ladies spoke so to their inferiors, but this fashion had ceased with Louis XV.

If I did not enjoy my stay at Raincy much, I did when I was at Gennevilliers, which made up for it; this place then belonged to the Comte de Vaudreuil, a most charming person. It was not a pretty place, and had been bought on account of the Comte d'Artois, because of there being plenty of hunting near, and the Comte de Vaudreuil had embellished it wonderfully. The house was tastefully furnished, but without magnificence; there was a small theater also, in which my sister-in-law's brother, M. de Rivière, and myself often acted comic operettas, along with Mme Dugazon, Garat, Cailleau, and Laruette. These two last had retired from the stage, but were admirable actors, and so natural that when they were repeating the scene of the two fathers in *Rose and Colas*, I believed they were talking together and said, "Come, do begin the rehearsal."

The last play acted in the theater at Gennevilliers was a representation of the *Marriage de Figaro*, by the actors from the Comédie-Française. I remember that Mlle Sainval was the countess and Mlle Olivier the page; Beaumarchais must have worried the Comte de Vaudreuil into permitting such a very doubtful play to be performed in this theater. The dialogues, couplets, all were against the court, of which most of the audience was composed, not to speak of the presence of our excellent prince. Everyone felt this want of tact; but Beaumarchais was wild with delight. He rushed about like a madman, and on someone complaining of the heat, he did not give time for the windows to be opened but broke all the panes with his cane, which annoyed everyone still more.

The Comte de Vaudreuil must have repented having accorded his protection to the author of the *Marriage de Figaro*. In fact, shortly after this representation Beaumarchais requested an audience, which he obtained at once, and he came to Versailles at such an early hour that the count was barely out of bed. He then began to speak of some financial project which he had conceived, and which he said would work wonders; and then he wound up by proposing to give the Comte de Vaudreuil a considerable sum if he would undertake the guidance of the affair. "Monsieur de Beaumarchais," he replied, "you could not have arrived at a luckier time; for I have passed a good night, I have digested well, and never felt better in my life. Had you come to me yesterday with such a proposition I should have thrown you out of the window."

One of the prettiest country seats I have seen was Villette. The Marquise de Villette, surnamed Good and Beautiful, having begged me to go and visit them, I spent some days at that place; we came upon a man one day who was painting some railings in the lovely park; he was so expeditious that M. de Villette complimented him on it. "As for me," he replied, "I would undertake to efface in a day all that Rubens painted in his life."

Some time before the Revolution I went to Morfontaine, and from thence we made an excursion to Ermenonville, where I saw the tomb of J. J. Rousseau. The notoriety of this fine park spoiled the excursion for me; at each turn so many inscriptions are noticed that all one's ideas are destroyed. M. de Morfontaine received with so much kindness and simplicity that everyone seemed at their ease with him. The Comte de Vaudreuil, Le Brun (the poet), the Chevalier de Coigny, Brongniart, Robert Riviére, and my brother acted charades every evening, and kept waking each other up to tell them; this mirth shows how much liberty was permitted in that place. In real truth, order was as much banished as restraint. Fortunately we were all intimate, and not a large party, for I never saw a château worse kept.

On leaving Morfontaine for Maupertuis, one could not help comparing the difference between these two fine houses. At Maupertuis all was order and magnificence. M. de Montesquiou kept up all the state of a great personage. As he was equerry to Monsieur and had been so since the death of Louis XV, it was easy for him to put carriages and horses at our disposal. The mother and wife of M. de Montesquiou were very good to me. His sister-in-law, who afterward became governess to the son of Napoleon, was kind, natural, and very amiable. As for him, I have often seen him at Paris, and he struck me as being witty but cold; at Maupertuis he was not like the same man. I remember one evening when we were rather a small party, the Marquis de Montesquiou told us our fortunes. He foretold me that I should live long, and be an amiable old lady because I was not a coquette. Now I have lived a long time, but am I an amiable old lady? I doubt it; but at least I am a loving one.

Adieu.

LETTER X

Dear friend, I dined several times at Saint-Ouen with the Duc de Nivernais, who had a fine place there and who entertained a great deal. He was always renowned for the ease of his manner and was distinguished by his extreme politeness toward women of all ages. It is very difficult nowadays to give any idea of the urbanity and graceful ease of the manners of forty years ago, which then were the great charm of Parisian society. This politeness of which I speak has totally disappeared. Women reigned then; the Revolution dethroned them.

I dined often with the Maréchal de Noailles in his lovely château at the entrance to Saint-Germain. He was very pleasant; his wit and gaiety communicated itself to all his guests, whom he selected from among the most distinguished literary characters and court celebrities. The Maréchal de Noailles had an original and very piquant mind. He rarely resisted a desire to say something cutting; it was he who replied to Louis XV, when eating some olives out hunting, which he found bad: "They are from the bottom of the cask, Sire, no doubt."

This speech carries me back to a woman of whom I have not yet spoken, a woman who, though belonging to the lowest ranks of society, passed through a king's palace, and from thence to the scaffold, and whose sad end makes one forgive the scandal attached to her life. It was in 1786 that I went for the first time to Louveciennes, where I had promised to take the portrait of

Mme du Barry. I was extremely curious to see this favorite of whom I had so often heard. Mme du Barry must then have been about forty-five, she was tall, but not too much so, stout, with a full but beautiful figure; her face was still charming, with regular and pleasing features; her hair was fair and curly, like a child's; her complexion was the only part which was becoming withered. She received me very gracefully and seemed to me to have good manners, but I found her mind more natural than her manners; her glances were those of a coquette, for her long eyes were never opened wide, and her pronunciation was childish and did not agree well with her age. She gave me an apartment behind the weir at Marly, whose dismal noise worried me dreadfully. Underneath my apartment was a gallery, in which were placed, without any sort of order, busts, vases, columns, the rarest and most precious marbles, and quantities of other rare and valuable objects, all massed together in confusion, so that one might have believed oneself in the house of the mistress of several sovereigns, who had all enriched her with their gifts. These remains of magnificence contrasted strangely with the simplicity adopted by the mistress of the house, both in her toilette and manner of living.

In summer as in winter, Mme du Barry wore only white muslin or percale dressing gowns, and every day, no matter what the weather was like, she walked in her park or outside without feeling any ill effects, so much strengthened was she by her country life. She did not keep up any intercourse with the large court which had for so long surrounded her.

In the evenings we were often alone, seated by the fire, Mme du Barry and myself. She often talked to me about Louis XV and his court, always with the greatest respect for the one and very cautiously about the other. But she avoided all details; it was evident that she preferred not to mention this subject, so that as a rule her conversation was rather flat. Otherwise she was a good woman both in words and action; she was very benevolent and succored all the poor at Louveciennes. We often went together and visited some poor person, and I remember even now how justly angry she was when at the bedside of a woman who had a baby and was in great want.

Every day we took our coffee after dinner in the pavillion, so renowned for the taste and richness of its ornamentation. The first time I saw it, Mme du Barry said, "It was in this room that Louis XV did me the honor to dine; above it there was tribune for the musicians and singers who played and sang during the repast." When, before the Terror, Mme du Barry went to England to seek for her stolen diamonds, which she found there, the English had received her cordially and did their utmost to prevent her returning to France; in fact at the last her friends unharnessed her post-horses to make her stay; it was only her desire to join the Duc de Brissac, who she had left concealed at Louveciennes, which made her resist the instances of her friends to keep her in London, where she might have lived in ease from the sale of her diamonds. Unfortunately for her, she quitted England and rejoined the Duc de Brissac at Louveciennes. Shortly after, the duke was arrested before her eyes and taken to prison at Orleans. From thence they fetched him and three others, to lead to Versailles, as they said; all four were put in a tumbril and had barely got halfway there when they were shamefully massacred!

The bleeding head of the Duc de Brissac was carried to Mme du Barry. You can imagine what that unhappy woman must have felt at the sight! It was not long before she experienced the same fate, reserved for everybody who possessed any fortune or a great name. She was betrayed by a little *nègre* called Zamor, of whom mention is made in the memoirs of those times, as having been most kindly treated both by her and by Louis XV. Arrested and imprisoned, Mme du Barry was judged and condemned to death by the Revolutionary Tribunal at the end of 1793. She is the only woman, among the numbers of women who perished in those days, who was unable to face the scaffold; she wept, she implored mercy from the horrible crowd which surrounded her, and that crowd was so affected by her entreaties that the executioner hastened to put an end to her agony. I am convinced that had the victims of that awful time not died so courageously, the Terror would have ceased much sooner. Men whose intellects are not fully developed have too little imagination to feel touched by internal suffering, and the pity of the populace is more easily aroused than its admiration.

I made three portraits of Mme du Barry. In the first place I represented her in a peignoir, with a straw hat; in the second she is robed in white satin, holding a crown in one hand and with one arm resting on a pedestal. I painted this picture very carefully; it was destined for the Duc de Brissac, as was the other also, and I have seen it recently. The old general to whom it belonged had the head touched up, for it is not like the one I did; this one is rouged up to the eyes, and Mme du Barry never wore any at all. I renounce therefore any connection with this head, which is not mine; the rest of the painting is intact and well preserved. It was sold at the death of the above mentioned general.

The third portrait I made of Mme du Barry is in my own house; I commenced it toward the end of 1789. I had painted the head and traced out the bust and arms, when I was obliged to return to Paris; I hoped to be able to go back again to Louveciennes and finish my work, but Berthier and Foullon had just been assassinated. My terror was very great and I only thought of how to leave France; I therefore left this picture unfinished. I do not know by what chance the Comte Louis de Narbonne became the possessor during my absence; on my return to France he restored it to me, and I have just completed it.

The sad contents of this letter warn me that I have arrived at a period of my existence of which I could wish to lose all knowledge and all memory, had I not promised you a sincere and complete recital of my life; no more gaiety, Greek suppers, or comedies, but days of anguish and fear, which I shall relate in my next letters.

Adieu, dear friend.

LETTER XI

I cannot recall the last visits I made without some unpleasant memories mingling with those of happier moments: in 1788, for instance, I went with Robert to spend a few days at Romainville, with the Maréchal de Ségur. During our journey we noticed that the peasants no longer took off their hats, on the contrary, they looked sullenly at us, and some even menaced us with their sticks. When we reached our destination we were witnesses of a most terrible storm. Mme de Ségur and myself gazed at each other; we seemed to foresee that gloomy day, the evils of which without being a fortune teller one could easily have foretold. The evening and the next day we all went with the maréchal to behold the ravages made by the storm. Wheat, vines, and fruit trees had been completely destroyed. The peasants were weeping and wringing their hands. Everyone did their utmost to succor these unfortunate creatures; the larger landowners gave away sums of money—one very rich man distributed forty thousand francs among the sufferers; to the shame of humanity, be it said, that he was one of the first who were massacred by the bloodthirsty revolutionists.

In June 1789, I was dining at Malmaison and met the Abbé Sièyes and several other partisans of the Revolution. M. du Molay ranted against the aristocracy; everybody yelled and declaimed on different topics, enough to have created a general disturbance; it was like a revolutionary club, and these conversations made me very uncomfortable. After dinner Abbé Sièyes observed to someone, "I really believe we shall go too far." "They will go so far that they will lose their way," said I, to Mme du Molay, who had heard what the Abbé had said and felt distressed at such sinister forebodings.

About the same time I went to spend a few days at Marly with Mme Auguié, a sister of Mme Campan, and attached to the Queen's household like herself. She had a château and fine park near the weir. One day as we were standing at a window looking on to the court, and from thence to the high road we saw a drunken man enter and fall down. Mme Auguié, with her usual kindness, called to her husband's valet and told him to pick up this unfortunate creature, take him to the kitchen, and look after him. Soon after the valet returned. "Madame is really too kind," said he, "this man is a miscreant! Here are the papers he let fall from his pocket." And he placed in our hands several documents, of which one began with "Down with the royal family! Down with the nobles and priests!" then followed revolutionary litanies and thousands of atrocious prophecies, drawn up in language which made one's hair stand on end. Mme Auguié had the village guards called up; four of these soldiers came; she desired them to take this man away and find out more about him. They led him off, but the valet, who followed them for some distance, without their knowledge, saw them, as soon as they were out of sight, take their prisoner by the arm and jump, sing, and dance with him as though they were the best of friends. This terrified us;

what was to become of us if the civil guard even lent itself to the cause of the wicked? I advised Mme Auguié to show these papers to the Queen, and a few days after, being on duty again, she read them to Her Majesty, who returned them, saying, "It is impossible that they should meditate such wickedness. I shall never believe them capable of it!" Alas! subsequent events have shown the fallacy of this noble doubt; and, not to speak of the august victim who would not believe in such horrors, poor Mme Auguié herself was destined to pay for her devotion with her life. This devotion never wavered. In the worst times of the Revolution, knowing the Queen was without money, she insisted on lending her twenty-five louis. The revolutionists heard of it and went to the Tuileries to take her to prison, or in other words to the guillotine. When she beheld them coming furiously toward her with menaces on their lips, Mme Auguié preferred a speedy death to the agony of falling into their hands; she threw herself out of the window and was killed.

Mme Auguié had two sisters; one was the Mme Campan, well known as first lady in waiting to the Queen, and the clever directress of the educational establishment at Saint-Germain, where all the celebrities of the empire had their daughters educated. I knew Mme Campan at Versailles. I never doubted that she would ever feel grateful to her august mistress for her kindness, when, during my sojourn at St. Petersburg, you must remember that one evening I heard her accused of having abandoned and betrayed the Queen. I stood up warmly for her against this calumnious report, and repeatedly said that it could not be true.

I shall resume in my next letter the account of the sad events which caused me to flee from my country and seek for safety in foreign lands. Adieu, dear friend.

LETTER XII

The dreadful year of 1789 began, and fear had taken hold of the wisest among us. I remember one evening having invited some friends for a concert, and they arrived with consternation depicted on their faces; they had been that morning to Longchamps; the populace, assembled at the Barrière de l'Etoile, had abused them horribly, especially those who were driving—some wretches sprang on to the carriage steps calling out, "Next year you will be behind your carriages, and we shall be inside!" The person least terrified was Mme de Villette, Voltaire's beauty. As for me, I had no occasion to be told of fresh details on the horrors which were being prepared. I know well that my house, rue du Gros-Chenet, where I had not lived for more than three months, was marked by the miscreants. They threw sulfur into our cellars through the gratings. If I stood at the window, brutal *sansculottes* shook their fists at me. I heard all sorts of sinister rumors on every side and lived in a continual state of anxiety and despair.

My health suffered so much that two good friends, Brongniart, the architect, and his wife, when they came to see me, found me looking so ill and thin that they implored me to come and spend a few days with them, which offer I accepted with gratitude. Brongniart lodged in the Invalides. So much care ought to have done me good, seeing too that my friends did not think as badly of affairs as I did; but they could not reassure me against the evils I foresaw. What was the use of living? or of taking care of oneself? said I often to my friends, for terror of the future made me take a disgust to life, and yet my liveliest imagination never went as far as the reality. Afterward I remember having supper with Brongniart and the excellent M. de Sombreuil, then governor of the Invalides, being one of the guests; he told us that they were coming to take possession of the arms at the depot, but added that he had hidden them so well that he defied them to discover them. The worthy man did not know that the only person to be relied on was oneself. As the arms were taken away, he was of course betrayed by one of the inmates of the establishment whom he had employed.

M. de Sombreuil, as much respected for his moral qualities as for his military talents, was imprisoned with those who were massacred in the prisons on the second of September. The assassins spared his life owing to the tears and supplications of his heroic daughter, but atrocious even in their mercy they forced Mlle de Sombreuil to drink a glass of the blood that was flowing in the prison; and for long afterward the sight of anything red would make the unfortunate girl retch dreadfully! Later on in 1794, M. de Sombreuil was sent to the scaffold by the Revolutionary Tribunal.

I had quite decided on leaving France. I had long desired to go to Rome. The number of portraits I had undertaken had alone prevented my doing so before; but if ever the time for my departure was to come it had come then, I could no longer paint! My imagination was so dazed by the horrors I saw that it ceased to influence my art: and besides, wicked libels were showered on my friends and on myself, alas! And although, thank God!, I had done harm to no one, I was in the place of the man who said, "I am accused of having taken away the towers of Notre Dame; they are in their places; but go I must, for it is plain I have given offense somehow."

I left several unfinished portraits, among others that of Mlle Contat; I refused to paint Mlle de Laborde, afterward Duchesse de Noailles, whose father desired her portrait. It was no longer a question of success or fortune; it was a question of saving one's head. Therefore I had my carriage packed and had my passport for leaving the next day with my daughter and her governess, when my room was entered by a number of armed National Guards, most of them drunk and with dreadful countenances. Some came up to me and spoke in coarse language, and said, "You shall not leave, *citoyenne*." At last they departed. I was left in a most miserable condition, when I saw two return whose faces did not terrify me; although they were of the band, I soon perceived they meant no harm. "Madame," said one, "we are your neighbors, we advise you to leave as quickly as possible. You cannot live here, you are so altered that we are quite concerned for you. But do not leave in your carriage; go by the stagecoach, it is much safer." I thanked them heartily and followed their good advice. I was so altered that, the eve of my departure, having gone to see my mother to wish her goodbye, she only recognized me from my voice; yet it was only three weeks since we had met.

At last the welcome day arrived, it was the fifth of October. The King and Queen were brought from Versailles to Paris amid pikes! My brother witnessed the arrival of their Majesties at the Hôtel de Ville. Never, said he, had the Queen looked more majestic than today, when she entered amid these demons. Then he told me the beautiful answer she had made to M. Bailly: "I know all, I have seen all, and I forgive all." The events of that day caused me great anxiety on account of their Majesties and for all decent people, so that at midnight I was dragged to the stagecoach in a most miserable state of mind. I feared passing the faubourg Saint-Antoine, which I was forced to do, to reach the Barrière du Trone. My brother Robert and my husband accompanied me to the barrière. This faubourg, of which we were so fearful, was perfectly quiet; all its inhabitants, workmen and others, had been to Versailles to fetch the royal family, and the fatigue of the journey had made them sleepy.

I had in front of me in the stagecoach a very dirty and odoriferous man, who quietly informed me he had stolen several watches and other objects. Fortunately, he saw nothing on me likely to tempt him; for I took but little linen with me, and eighty louis for my journey. I left all my trinkets at Paris, and the proceeds of my labors were in my husband's possession, who, as I have said before, spent it all. I lived, while abroad, on the portraits I took. Far from M. Le Brun ever sending me money, he wrote me most dismal letters on his poverty, so that I once sent him a thousand écus, and another time a hundred louis, besides sending equal sums to my mother.

The thief, not content with relating his robberies, spoke continually about hanging such and such people, naming several of my acquaintances. My little girl thought him very wicked and was much afraid of him, which gave me courage to say, "I pray you, Sir, do not speak of murder before this child!" He was silenced and amused himself by playing with her. There was, besides this man, another, a furious Jacobin from Grenoble. In all the towns, crowds stopped the stagecoach to learn news of Paris. Our Jacobin then called out, "We have the Baker and his wife safe in Paris; they will be forced to accept a constitution, and all will be well!" The people believed in this man as an oracle. I no longer feared for myself, but for everybody—my mother, brother, and friends; I trembled also for their Majesties. All along the road as far as Lyons, men on horseback approached the stagecoach to tell us the King and Queen were massacred, and Paris was on fire. My poor little girl trembled all over; she believed her father was killed, and our house burned down, and when I had succeeded in calming her, there came another horseman with the same tales.

I wore the dress of a badly dressed workwoman, with a large handkerchief falling over my eyes. I had had occasion to be thankful I had taken this precaution on my journey. I had exhibited at the *Salon* the portrait representing myself with my child in my arms. The Grenoble

Jacobin spoke of the exhibition and praised this same picture. I trembled lest he should recognize me and did my best to hide my face. Thanks to that and my dress, I escaped unnoticed.

I cannot tell you what I felt when we crossed the Bridge of Beauvoisin. Then, and then only, I began to breathe freely. I was out of France—my country—which I reproached myself for quitting with so much joy. The sight of the mountains distracted me from my sad thoughts. I had never seen high ones before. Those of Savoy seemed to reach the sky.

I ascended the Mont Cenis, along with several other strangers. A postillion came up. "Madame ought to take a mule," said he, "for a lady like herself." I told him I was a workwoman, accustomed to walking. "Ah," replied he, laughing. "Madame is not a workwoman. I know who she is." "And who am I, then?" "You are Madame Le Brun, who paints beautifully, and we are very glad to know you are safe away from wicked people." I never could guess how this man managed to know my name, but that has proved to me how many emissaries the Jacobins must have employed. Happily, I no longer feared them; I was out of their dreadful clutches. For want of my country, I was going to inhabit places where peace and the arts flourished. I was going to visit Rome, Naples, Berlin, Vienna, and St. Petersburg, and, above all, I was going, unknown to myself, to meet you, dear friend.

Always yours.

Souvenirs

After having crossed the Mount Cenis, I reached Turin, tired in body and mind. The next day, very early, I acquainted Porporati of my arrival; his beautiful engravings are well known. We went to the largest theater, and there I perceived in the front boxes the Duc de Bourbon and the Duc d'Enghien, whom I had not seen for some time. The music pleased me extremely, and I asked Porporati if his city contained many lovers of art; he shook his head and said: "They know nothing about it. This is what happened to me: a very great man, having heard that I was an engraver, came to me quite recently and wanted me to engrave his seal." This little anecdote convinced me that the inhabitants of Turin had no very great knowledge of art either.

I left my kind hosts for Parma; I had barely arrived there when I received a visit from the Comte de Flavigny, staying there as Minister of Louis XVI. M. de Flavigny made me see everything of any importance in Parma. After having contemplated the magnificent painting by Correggio of the Nativity, which we have had in the Musée du Louvre, I visited the churches where the works of this great master are the finest ornament. I could not behold so many divine paintings without believing in the inspiration which the Christian artist draws from his religion; no doubt fables have charming fictions, but the poetry of Christianity is to me far more beautiful.

I went to the summit of the church of Saint John; there I was able to admire more closely a cupola where Correggio painted several angels, surrounded by feathery clouds. What surprised me was that the faces are so exquisitely finished, they might have been standing on a painter's easel, and yet it does not detract from the view of the cupola seen from below.

My wish was to spend at least a week Bologna, in order to admire the masterpieces of its school, generally considered one of the first in Italy. I visited several of the palaces, and in one of these the *custode* followed me round and persisted in telling me the names of all the painters. He irritated me much, and I quietly told him he was giving himself needless trouble, for I knew all these masters. He contented himself after that with accompanying me; but as he heard me admiring the finest works and repeating the painters' names, he left me and went to my servant and said: "Who is this lady? I have led many great princesses through this gallery, but I never met any as well informed as this one is." Three days after my arrival, the third of November, 1789, I was received as a member of the Academy of Bologna. M. Bequetti, who was the director, came himself to bring my letters of acceptation.

I consoled myself for leaving so many beautiful things by the idea of those which I should find in Florence. As soon as I entered the illustrious city, I was surprised and delighted with its beauty and view. Notwithstanding my extreme haste to get to Rome, I felt obliged to remain for some time in this city. I visited the celebrated gallery which the Medicis enriched with so much care; but I should require a volume to enter into details on all the riches I had the pleasure of beholding in this place of enchantment for artists. Of course, I could not leave Florence without seeing the Altoviti Palace, where Raphael's fine portrait by himself is kept. This portrait has been put under glass, in order to preserve it, and this precaution has darkened the shadows, but all the flesh tints are very pure and delicately colored. The features of the portrait are very regular, good eyes and a clear, penetrating expression.

The day I visited the gallery containing the portraits of modern painters by themselves, I was honored by being asked for mine for the City of Florence, and I promised to send it when in Rome.

Very soon after my arrival in Rome I painted my portrait for the Florentine Gallery. I depicted myself, with a palette in my hand, before a picture on which I was supposed to be tracing the head of our Queen with white chalks. Then I painted Miss Pitt, a daughter of Lord Camelford; she was sixteen and very pretty, therefore I represented her as Hebe on clouds, holding a goblet in her hand from which an eagle was drinking. I painted the eagle from life and had great doubts whether he would not devour me; he belonged to Cardinal de Bernis. The wretched creature, who was accustomed to living chained up in a courtyard in the open air, was furious at being in my room and wished to fly at me. I confess I felt horribly frightened.

At the same time I took the portrait of a Polish lady, the Countess Potocka. I painted her very picturesquely, leaning against a mossy rock and behind her some waterfalls. I afterward took the portrait of Mlle Roland, then mistress of Lord Wellesley, who married her soon after; then my own portrait on my reception to the Rome Academy, a copy of which I destined for Florence; a portrait of Lord Bristol, half length; and that of Mme Silva. In fact I worked prodigiously hard at Rome and during the three years I passed in Italy. Not only did I find painting a great resource and enjoyment, surrounded as I was by works of art; but I had to rebuild my fortune, for I did not have a hundred francs to my name. Luckily I had only to choose among the greatest personages the portraits I wished to take.

One of my delights while in Rome was the music, and certainly I had plenty. The celebrated Banti was there during my stay; although she had sung several times in Paris I had never heard her, and I had this pleasure at a concert. Shortly after my arrival, I went with Angelica Kauffmann to see the opera *Cesar*, in which Crescentini made his debut. His singing and voice were perfection; he took a woman's part, and was clothed with a panier, like those worn at the Court of Versailles, which made us laugh heartily.

There is no city in the world where life passes so agreeably as in Rome; to walk within its walls is a pleasure, for one never tires of visiting again and again the Coliseum, the Capitol, the Pantheon, Saint Peter's with its piazza, its superb obelisk, its noble fountain which the sun lights up so exquisitely with rainbow hues. This piazza has a most wonderful appearance at sunset and by moonlight. I am told that all the lower class of women wear daggers; the men I know are never without them, and this custom often leads to serious results. One evening, shortly after my arrival in Rome, hearing a great noise and tumult in the street, I sent to inquire the cause, and was informed that a man had just been stabbed from motives of revenge. It is only among themselves, however, that they give way to the violence of their passions, visitors to Rome being quite safe. The manners of the higher classes are, however, much more gentle, for society is the same as in the other cities of Europe. Besides I am not a good judge, for with the exception of what concerns my art, and the invitations which I received to numberless reunions, I had little opportunity of knowing the "grandes dames" in Rome. It occurred to me, as it naturally does to all exiles, to seek in a foreign city the society of my compatriots. During the years 1789 and 1790, Rome was crowded with French émigrés, many of whom were old acquaintances. Among them I must mention the Duc and Duchesse de Fitz-James, with their sons; also the Polignacs. I did not care to visit this family often, for fear of exciting calumnious remarks, for it would at once have been said I was plotting with them; and I thought it a duty to avoid them as much as possible, on account of the relations and friends I had left in France.

Of all the French ladies in Rome, I admired the beautiful Duchesse de Fleury the most; she was quite young, and nature had lavished on her all her choicest gifts. She had a lovely face, and the figure of a Venus; added to this, her mind was of a superior order. We felt mutually drawn toward each other; she loved art, and like myself, was passionately fond of the beauties of nature; I found in her a companion I had often longed for.

The arrival in Rome of so many persons who brought news from France made me experience the most varied emotions, sometimes sad and sometimes gay. I was told, for example, that, shortly after my departure, the King having been requested to let his portrait be taken, replied: "No, I shall wait the return of Madame Le Brun to have my portrait taken, and it shall be a companion to the one she did of the Queen; I will be painted full-length standing, and giving an order to Monsieur de la Pérouse to make a voyage round the world."

Nothing gratifies me more than to recall the kindness Louis XVI always showed to me, and I always reproach myself that I hitherto have forgotten to mention that at the time I made the great picture of the Queen with her children, M. d'Angiviller came to tell me that the King wished to give me the order of Saint-Michel, which was a decoration entirely for male artists and learned men of the highest order. As even at that time the most odious calumnies were circulated about me, I feared that so great a distinction would carry to its height the envy already excited, and, though deeply grateful, I nevertheless begged M. d'Angiviller to try to induce the King to renounce the idea of according me this favor.

I met in Rome one of my best and oldest friends, M. d'Agincourt, who, when living in Paris, lent me all the beautiful drawings in his possession to copy. M. d'Agincourt was an enthusiastic lover of art, and above all of painting.

The Abbé Maury, who was not then a cardinal, came to tell me that the Pope wished me to take his portrait. I greatly desired to do so, but it was necessary that I should be veiled while painting His Holiness, and the fear that under the circumstance I should not be able to do justice to my subject compelled me to decline this honor. I was very sorry about it, for Pius VI was one of the handsomest men I had seen.

All artists must feel as I did, that it is impossible to walk round Rome without feeling the desire to use one's pencil; I have never made the smallest excursion, not even a walk, without bringing back some sketches I have made.

It was with regret I left this place of splendor and ruin. Ah! what thoughts it gives rise to, and how our greatest works crumble into decay. Since the beginning of the world the marvels of the heavens alone remain unchanged. How can one feel pride, when each step that one takes in the environs of Rome reveals the instability of earthly things; for there one tramples underfoot the *chefs-d'œuvre* of antiquity.

I had been in Rome for nearly eight months when, seeing that all the visitors were leaving for Naples, I decided on going there also. I cannot express the admiration I felt on entering this city. The brilliant sunshine, the sea and the islands which one perceives in the distance, Vesuvius, from whose summit rose a dense column of smoke, and then the population so animated, so noisy, and which differs so entirely from that of Rome that one might imagine the two cities were a thousand miles apart.

I had scarcely arrived when the Russian ambassador to Naples, the Count Skavronsky, sent one of his servants to inquire after me, and immediately afterward sent me in a sumptuous dinner. Count Skavronsky had very noble and regular features; he was very pale. The countess was gentle and lovely as an angel; the famous Potemkin, her uncle, had loaded her with riches of which she made no use. Her happiness was to lie stretched on a sofa, wrapped in a large black pelisse, and wearing no stays. Her mother-in-law ordered for her from Mlle Bertin, *marchande de modes* to the Queen Marie Antoinette, boxes full of the most exquisite dresses. I do not believe the countess ever looked at them, and when her mother-in-law entreated her to wear them, she answered carelessly, "What is the use? For whom? For what?" She made me the same answer on showing me her jewel case, one of the richest imaginable; it contained enormous diamonds that had been given her by Potemkin, and which I had never seen her wear. In the daytime she remained constantly idle; she was quite uneducated and had no conversation: in spite of all this, thanks to her lovely face and angelic sweetness, she possessed an invincible charm.

Count Skavronsky had made me promise to paint his wife before anyone else at Naples; I agreed, and two days after my arrival, I commenced the portrait of the ambassadress almost full-length, holding in her hand a medallion in which was the portrait of her husband. I had given my first sitting when I received a visit from the English ambassador, Sir William Hamilton, who begged as a favor that the first portrait I took at Naples should be that of a beautiful woman he presented to me; it was Mrs. Hart, his mistress, who shortly afterward became Lady Hamilton, and whose beauty has made her celebrated. I painted Mrs. Hart as a bacchante reposing on the seashore and holding in her hand a cup. Her lovely face was very animated and was a complete contrast to that of the countess; she had an enormous quantity of beautiful chestnut hair, which when loose covered her entirely—thus as a bacchante she was perfect.

Sir William Hamilton had this portrait done for himself; but I must mention that he frequently sold his pictures when he found he could make money on them, which caused the eldest son of our ambassador at Naples, M. de Talleyrand, to say one day on hearing that Sir William Hamilton was a patron of art, "Say rather it is art who is his patron." The truth is that after having bargained a long time for the portrait of his mistress, he got me to do it for one hundred louis, which was twenty-four hundred francs, and that he sold it afterward in

London for three hundred guineas, or in French money eight thousand francs.

The life of Lady Hamilton is a romance. Her mother is reported to have been only a poor servant. Having heard of a tavern much frequented by artists, Lady Hamilton decided on going there to seek for employment. In this situation she soon fell away from the path of virtue, and after being abandoned by different lovers, found herself reduced to the lowest stage of degradation. A strange chance drew her out of the abyss. A Dr. Graham hired her to show her at his house, under the name of the Goddess of Health; she was covered with only a thin veil. Crowds of people went to see her; artists especially were charmed with her. Some time after this exhibition, a painter by the name of Romney took her as his model; he put her in a thousand graceful attitudes and placed her in his pictures. It was there she acquired that habit of being able to change her expression in a moment, which afterward made her so celebrated.

The Duc de Berry and the Duc de Bourbon, having heard of her attitudes, expressed a great wish to see her perform, which she had always declined doing in London. I begged her to give me an evening for the two princes. I also invited a few other Frenchmen who I knew were very curious to witness the scene; and I placed in the center of my drawing room a very large frame, enclosed on the right and left by two screens. I had arranged the light so as to shine on Lady Hamilton, as one would light up a picture. Everyone having arrived, Lady

Hamilton went through numerous attitudes inside the frame, in a truly admirable manner.

I was delighted with my residence at the Hotel Morocco, to say nothing of my kind friends being so near me. From my windows I reveled in the most magnificent view and the gayest thoroughfare. The sea, with the island of Capri in front of me, Vesuvius to the left, which promised an eruption from the quantity of smoke emitted; to the right the hill of Posillipo, covered with beautiful villas, and superb vegetation, then the quay of the Chiaia always so animated, and which presented so many amusing pictures; sometimes it was the *lazzaroni* who came to quench their thirst at the fountain in front of my windows, where the young washerwomen came to wash their clothes; on Sundays it was the young peasants, in their finest costumes, who danced the tarantella before my house, playing the tambourine; and every evening I could see the fishermen with their torches, whose light was reflected in the sea.

Immediately on my arrival at Naples, I called on M. le Baron de Talleyrand, then French ambassador to the court, who showed me every kindness throughout my stay there. I found the amiable Portuguese Mme Silva was still with him, and together we planned numerous excursions. I also visited Paestum, and though the distance from Naples is only twenty-five leagues, the journey is very fatiguing; but I felt capable of braving anything for the satisfaction of admiring monuments which are between three and four thousand years old. Of the three temples still standing, that of Juno was in a beautiful state of preservation; from the exterior one might imagine it to be quite perfect. This temple is noble and imposing, as is everything belonging to the ancients, near whom we are but pygmies.

These excursions and many others did not prevent my painting a great deal at Naples. I had undertaken so many portraits that on my first visit to that city I remained six months, though I had only intended remaining six weeks. M. le Baron de Talleyrand came one morning to announce that the Queen of Naples wanted me to take the portraits of her two eldest daughters, which I commenced without delay. Her Majesty was on the point of leaving for Vienna for the purpose of arranging the marriages of the princesses. I recollect that on her return she said to me, "I had a prosperous journey, for I have happily settled two marriages for my daughters." The eldest married the emperor of Austria, Francis II, and the second, who was called Luisa, married the grand duke of Tuscany. This last one was very ugly and made such dreadful faces that I did not wish to finish her portrait. She died a few years after her marriage.

When the Queen was gone, I painted the prince royal also. The hour for my sittings at the palace was always at noon, and to get there I had to pass along the Chiaia at the hottest time of the day. The houses to the left, facing the sea, are all painted pure white, and the glare of the sun on them nearly blinded me. To save my eyes I decided on wearing a green veil, which, as I had never seen one worn by anyone previously, must have appeared very singular, for the veils then worn were either white or black; but a few days afterward I noticed several Englishwomen imitated me, and green veils became the fashion. I found the benefit of my green veil when at St. Petersburg, where the snow is so dazzling I should have lost my sight.

At this time I commenced the portrait of Paisiello. While giving me a sitting he composed a piece of music, which was to be performed on the return of the Queen. I was charmed with this circumstance, as it enabled me to seize the traits of the great musician at the moment of inspiration.

All the portraits I had undertaken at Naples being finished, I returned to Rome. When shortly afterward meeting the Queen of Naples, who was returning from Vienna, she begged me with the most gracious and amiable manner to return to Naples in order to take her portrait. It was impossible to refuse, so I speedily put myself again en route.

Directly after my arrival in Naples, I had commenced the portrait of the Queen; this time the heat was so great that one day Her Majesty, who had given me a sitting, fell asleep, and I did the same. The Queen of Naples, without being as pretty as her youngest sister the Queen of France, resembled her very much; her face was worn, but one could see she had been handsome; her hands and arms were perfection as to color and form. This princess, who has had so much said and written against her, was in her own circle of a very affectionate disposition: her generosity was truly royal. She loved to minister to those in sorrow and was not afraid of mounting up to a fifth floor to give aid to the unfortunate. This was the noble woman against whom, under Bonaparte, were exhibited in the streets of Paris the most infamous and obscene engravings. It was necessary to calumniate her; they wanted her crown. One knows that she was betrayed by those whom she had always honored by her friendship and confidence. The woman whom she had loved best corresponded with the conqueror who succeeded, by underhand dealings, in dethroning the sister of Marie Antoinette, to put in her place Mme Murat.

The Queen of Naples had a noble disposition and was very clever. She bore the whole weight of the government. The King would not reign; he remained nearly always at Caserta, occupied by manufactures. At last, after having paid me munificently, as I was taking farewell of her, she gave me a beautiful box of old lacquered work marked with her initials, surrounded by very fine diamonds. This gift was worth ten thousand francs; but I shall never part with it.

I bade adieu to the beautiful bay of Naples, the charming hills of Posillipo and terrible Vesuvius with regret, and left for the third time to visit my dear Rome, and admire Raphael again in all his glory. When there, I undertook a great many portraits, which to tell the truth only partially satisfied me. I greatly regretted not having been able to employ my time, at either Naples or

Rome, in painting pictures of subjects which inspired me. I had been named a member of all the academies of Italy, which encouraged me to merit such flattering distinctions, and I was going to leave nothing in this lovely country which would add much to my reputation as an artist. These ideas were constantly on my mind—I have more than one sketch in my portfolio which could furnish the proof; but the want of money, as I had not one penny left of what I earned in France, and the natural weakness of my character, made me undertake engagements to the weary task of portrait painting. The result is that after having devoted my youth to work, with a constancy and assiduity very rare in a woman, loving my art as much as my life, I can scarcely count four works (portraits included) with which I am really pleased.

Many of the portraits which I took in Rome during my last stay there, however, procured me some gratification, among others that of seeing again Mesdames de France, the aunts of Louis XVI, who at once asked me to take their portraits. I was aware that a lady artist, who had always been inimical to me, had tried to injure me in the estimation of these princesses; but the extreme kindness with which they treated me assured me how little effect these vile calumnies had produced on them.

I left Rome on the fourteenth of April, 1792. On entering the carriage, I wept bitterly. I remained one day at Terni, and the following day continued our journey to Spoleto, where I saw that grand composition of Raphael, *The*

Adoration of the Kings. This picture, not being finished, clearly shows the method of the divine master. Raphael first painted the heads and hands; as for the draperies he tried different tints before painting them. After Spoleto, we stopped at Foligno. There I found another painting of Raphael, one of the most beautiful and original that he ever made; it represents the Virgin in the clouds, holding the infant Jesus in her arms. The infant is full of life and appears in relief; the Virgin is a noble figure; Saint John and the cardinal to the left of the picture are painted in the same style as Van Dyck, and the remaining figures are truly lifelike.

One souvenir of Florence, which I could not get rid of for a long time, was a visit I paid to the celebrated Fontana. This great anatomist had endeavored to represent, even to the smallest details, the interior of the human body. He showed me his cabinet, which was full of pieces of anatomy made in wax and flesh color. I looked around me with admiration, for it is impossible to consider the structure of the human body without being convinced of the existence of a god. I had experienced no disagreeable impression till I remarked a recumbent woman, life-size, and who one might have supposed was alive. Fontana told me to go close to the figure, and then lifting a sort of covering, he exhibited to my astonished gaze all the intestines arranged as our own. This sight had such an effect on me that I almost fainted. For several days I could think of nothing else, to the point that I could not see anyone without mentally stripping them of their clothes and skin, which put me in a deplorable nervous state. I asked M. Fontana for his advice to free me from this susceptibility; "I know too much, I see too much, and I feel it to my core," I told him. "What you regard as a weakness and a misfortune," he replied, "is your strength and it is your talent. If you want to minimize the disadvantages of your susceptibility, do not paint anymore." It will be easy to believe that I was not tempted to follow his advice; painting and living have never been more than one and the same word for me, and I have often given thanks to Providence for bestowing me my talent; and yet I had taken to complain like a fool to this famous anatomist.

I was longing to see Venice and arrived there on the eve of the Ascension. At first sight one might believe it was submerged, but soon the superb palaces, built in the gothic style, the walls of which are washed by the numerous canals, enchant the beholder by their wonderful and original effect. M. Denon, one of our most charming Frenchmen, conducted me first to the palace to see the *chefs-d'œuvre* which Venice possesses, and which are very numerous, and afterward the churches, which are full of the finest works of Tintoretto, Paolo Veronese, Bassano, and Titian. Having seen my Sybil, M. Denon begged me to let him exhibit it at his house, in order to show it to his acquaintances. It followed that many persons went to see this picture, which had a great success at Venice, to my infinite satisfaction. M. Denon also entreated me to take the portrait of his friend, Mme Marini, and I had great pleasure in doing so, for she had a lovely speaking face.

My desire being to return to France, I went to Turin with this intention. Mesdames de France, the aunts of Louis XVI, knowing that I must pass through Turin, had been good enough to give me letters to Mme Clotilde, their niece, Queen of Sardinia. They wrote that they greatly wished her to have her portrait taken by me; consequently, as soon as I was settled, I presented myself to Her Majesty. She received me kindly; at the same time she told me she was sorry to disoblige her aunts, but having entirely renounced the world, she would not be painted. What I saw of her myself entirely agreed with her words and vows; this princess had had her hair cut off and wore a little cap, which, as well as her dress, was of the simplest kind. Her thinness struck me so much the more, as I had seen her when very young before her marriage, and then her embonpoint was so prodigious that in France she went by the name of the "fat madame." After this interview I went to visit Madame, wife of Louis XVIII. Not only did she receive me most kindly, but she arranged many picturesque excursions for me in the environs of Turin with her lady-in-waiting, Mme de Gourbillon, and her son.

While inhabiting a farm six miles from Turin, I used to dream that the Revolution would soon cease, and that I should be able to return to France. Alas! it was in this peaceful abode that the cruelest blow struck me. The post brought me one evening a letter from my friend, M. de Rivière, my sister-in-law's brother, giving me information of the frightful occurrences of the tenth of August, with the most shocking details. I was thunderstruck; the lovely sky, the beautiful country, seemed all at once to be covered with a funereal gloom; in the anguish I endured, solitude became insupportable, and I decided on returning at once to Turin. On entering the city, my God! what did I see? The streets, the squares, crowded with men and women of all ages, who, flying from France, sought an asylum in Turin. They arrived by thousands, and it was a piteous spectacle. The greater number were destitute of everything, for they barely had time to escape with their lives. One of them, the Duchesse de Villeroi, then very aged, was entirely dependent on her maidservant, who had saved a small sum of money and who allowed her half a franc a day for her food. The King of Sardinia gave orders that these unfortunate people should be lodged and fed; but there was not room for all. One may imagine how much this cruel sight augmented my anxieties as to what was occurring in Paris, more particularly as M. de Rivière did not arrive, though he had written to tell me to expect him at Turin. At last, after much delay, he arrived, but so horribly changed that I could scarcely recognize him. The terrible scenes he had witnessed had affected both mind and body.

I scarcely dared to ask news of my mother, brother, and M. Le Brun. Nevertheless, M. de Rivière reassured me a little, by telling me my mother had not left Neuilly, that M. Le Brun remained quietly in Paris, and that my brother and his wife were in hiding.

In consequence of the disastrous news I heard from France, I gave up the idea of going there. I hired a small house in the environs of Turin. I went on painting. I painted a child bathing, after my daughter, and sold it at once to Prince Yusupov, who came to visit me.

Having decided on returning to Milan, and not knowing how to return in some measure the kindness Porporati had shown me, the idea occurred to me to take his daughter's portrait. He was so delighted that he had it engraved at once and gave me several proofs of it.

Halfway on the road to Milan, I was arrested for two days as a Frenchwoman. I wrote at once for a *permis de séjour*, which Count Wilczek, the Austrian ambassador, obtained for me. I went at once to thank him on my arrival and was received with much kindness. He pressed me to go to Vienna, where my presence, he assured me, would give great satisfaction. As the news I continued to receive from France obliged me to postpone indefinitely my return there, I at once decided on following his advice.

My reception at Milan was very flattering; the evening of my arrival I was serenaded by the young people of the best families. My first visit was to the refectory of the Church of the Grazia, to see the celebrated *Last Supper*, painted on the wall by Leonardo da Vinci. It is one of the masterpieces of the Italian school of painting; but it is in a sadly defaced condition, and I am told that during the last wars of Bonaparte in Italy, the soldiers amused themselves by shooting at it.

We arrived at last at the good city of Vienna, where two years and a half of my life passed in such an agreeable manner. Shortly after my arrival, I went to deliver in person the letters of introduction given me by Count Wilczek. Among the number was one for the celebrated Prince Kaunitz, who had been minister under Maria Theresa. I also called on the Comtesse de Thun. She invited me at once to her *soirées*, where all the best society in Vienna congregated. I met many émigrés from our poor France: the Duc de Richelieu, the Comte de Langeron, the Comtesse de Sabran and her son, the Polignac family, and, later on, the kind and good Comte de Vaudreuil, whom I was delighted to meet again. I have never seen assembled in any drawing room a greater number of pretty women than I met at Mme de Thun's. The greater number of these ladies brought their work and sat round a large table. Sometimes I was consulted as to the shading of their silks; but as what I detest more than anything else is to look at bright colors by lamp or candlelight, I very often gave my advice without looking.

It was always my custom, on arriving in a town, to make my first visits to the artists, and I did not delay in calling on Casanova, a celebrated painter of battle pieces. He was then working at several grand pictures, representing the noble deeds of Prince de Nassau. Casanova was full of spirit and originality. He was a great gossip, and he used to amuse us extremely at the dinners given by Prince Kaunitz, by stories which were sometimes pure fictions but very droll and comical. One day, the conversation turned on painting, and Rubens in particular, when someone, alluding to his immense talent, said that his general knowledge, which was also prodigious, had caused him to be named an ambassador. At these words, an old German baroness interrupted the speaker and said, "What! a painter, ambassador! No doubt it was an ambassador who amused himself by painting." "No, madame," replied Casanova, "it was a painter who amused himself by being an ambassador."

Shortly after my arrival in Vienna, I made the acquaintance of the Baron and Baroness Stroganov, who both asked me to take their portraits. The baroness was much liked for her sweetness and extreme benevolence. I have known very few men as amiable and gay as Baron Stroganov. When the desire for a good laugh and to amuse himself took him, he would invent all the follies imaginable. One day, knowing that many of his acquaintances and mine were going to see the exhibition of figures in wax, he excused himself under some pretext of being unable to accompany us, and going there before we did, he craftily placed himself behind a pedestal, in such a manner as only to show his head. Going through the portrait gallery, we passed before him, but he had fixed his eyes and features so immovably that none of us recognized him. At last, impatient at our want of notice, he moved and spoke. We were all frightened and much surprised at not having found him out.

I engaged apartments in Vienna itself, in which city it is said there are three causes of death: the wind, the dust, and the waltz. As soon as I was settled, I made many portraits, among others, the daughter of the Spanish ambassador and Mlle de Kageneck, who was sixteen and very pretty. My Sybil, which crowds came to my house to see, contributed not a little in deciding many people to ask me to paint them. It would be difficult for me to express all the gratitude I felt for the kindness I received in this city. Not only the Viennese showed affection for myself personally, but they also proved it by hanging my pictures in the best positions.

Vienna, whose extent is very considerable, as it comprises no less than thirty-two faubourgs, is full of fine palaces. The Imperial Museum contains pictures of the best masters. I went to several balls, particularly to those given by the Russian ambassador, Count Razumovsky, which may truly be called charming *fêtes*. They danced the waltz there with so much energy that I could not imagine all these persons did not fall from sheer giddiness; but both men and women are so accustomed to this violent exercise that they never rest as long as the ball continues.

I was a constant visitor at the house of the Countess Rumbeke, sister of Count Cobenzl, who collected in her drawing room the most distinguished society of Vienna. It was at her house I met Prince Metternich and his son, who since then has been made prime minister. I also met again the amiable Prince de Ligne; he related the charming journey he had made in the Crimea with the Empress Catherine II, which gave me a great desire to see this grand sovereign.

I learned nothing from the newspapers, for I had ceased to read them since the day I opened one at Mme de Rumbeke's, where I found the names of nine persons of my acquaintance who had been guillotined. It was from my brother that I heard of the horrible event, without adding any particulars. He merely said that Louis XVI and Marie Antoinette died on the scaffold! I have not ventured to ask the least question about all that accompanied or preceded this frightful assassination, so that to this day I know nothing except one incident.

When spring had set in, I took with me to the village of Huitzing the large portrait I was then painting of the Princesse de Liechtenstein, in order to finish it. This young princess had a beautiful figure, her pretty face had a sweet and celestial expression which gave me the idea of representing her as Iris. She was painted full-length, flying through the air. Her scarf was of the colors of the rainbow and floated carelessly around her. As may be imagined, I painted her feet naked; but when the picture was placed in the gallery of the prince, her husband, the heads of the family were greatly scandalized to perceive that the princess was exhibited without shoes, and the prince told me he had placed under the portrait a pretty little pair of shoes, which he told his grandparents had just slipped off and fallen to the ground.

I was as happy at Vienna as it was possible to be far from one's people and country. I had, therefore, no idea of leaving Austria before it was prudent and safe to return to France, when the Russian ambassador and many of my countrymen pressed me to go to St. Petersburg, where I was assured the empress would view my arrival with pleasure. I also thought that a short stay in Russia would complete the fortune I had promised to make before returning to Paris; I decided, therefore, on making the journey.

I reached St. Petersburg the twenty-fifth of July, 1795, by the Peterhof road, which gave me a favorable impression of the city; for the road is bordered on each side by charming country houses, surrounded by gardens in the English style. The inhabitants have done the best with their ground, which is very marshy, by ornamenting it with kiosks and little bridges over the canals. I was enchanted with the magnificence of this city, its monuments, its fine hotels and large streets. On one side of the river are superb monuments, that of the Academy of Arts, the Academy of Science, and many others, which are reflected in the Neva. In fact, St. Petersburg transported me to the time of Agamemnon, as much for the grandeur of its monuments as for the costume of its people, which recalls that of ancient times.

In the month of July, there was scarcely one hour of night; the sun sets at about half past ten in the evening; the reflection lasts till twilight sets in about half an hour after midnight.

I was far from feeling rested when, after having been in St. Petersburg only twenty-four hours, the Comte d'Esterházy was announced. He came to congratulate me on my arrival in St. Petersburg and told me that he should at once inform the empress of it and at the same time arrange for my presentation at court. That very evening M. d'Esterházy, on returning from Tsarskoye Selo, where the empress was residing, came to announce that

Her Majesty would receive me the following day at one o'clock. Such a prompt presentation, which I had not at all expected, threw me into extreme embarrassment; I had only some very plain muslin dresses, never wearing anything else in general, and it was impossible to have a handsome dress made by the following day even at St. Petersburg.

M. d'Esterházy gave me his arm, and we crossed a portion of the park when, at a window on the ground floor, I perceived a young person watering a pot of carnations. She looked about seventeen at the utmost; her features were fine and regular, and a perfect oval, her complexion was lovely, of a pallor quite in harmony with her face of angelic sweetness. She wore a white loose robe, fastened by a sash worn round her waist, which was small and supple as a young nymph's. Such as I have described her, this young person stepped forward so gracefully that I cried out, "She is Psyche!" It was the Princess Elizabeth, wife of Alexander. She at once addressed me and kept me sufficiently long enough to say a thousand gracious things, then she added, "We have long been wanting to see you here, madame, so much so that I even dreamed you had arrived." I left her with regret, and I have always remembered the lovely apparition.

Tremblingly, I arrived at the palace, and a few moments afterward was tête-à-tête with the autocrat of all the Russias. M. d'Esterházy had informed me that I must kiss her hand, and in consequence of this custom she had taken off one of her gloves, which ought to have reminded me of it; but I entirely forgot it. It is true that the appearance of this celebrated woman made such an impression on me that it was impossible to think of anything else but looking at her. I was at first extremely surprised to find her very short; I had fancied her prodigiously tall, as high as her grandeur. Genius seemed seated on her high white forehead. Her eyes were soft and sweet, her nose quite Grecian, her complexion florid, and her features very animated. She at once said in a voice of much sweetness, "I am charmed to see you here, madame; your reputation has preceded you. I greatly love the arts and, above all, painting. I am not a connoisseur, only an amateur." Shortly after my reception, Her Majesty expressed her intention of allowing me to pass the summer in this beautiful country palace. She ordered her controllers of the household to give me apartments in the château, desiring to have me near her in order to see me paint. Apart from the honor of finding myself lodged with the Sovereign, and the pleasure of living in such a beautiful place, I would have been irritated to be established at Tsarskoye Selo; because I have always had the greatest need to enjoy my freedom and to live according to my own taste, I have always infinitely preferred to live on my own.

My letters of introduction became quite useless to me; not only was I invited to pass my life in the best and most agreeable houses, but I met again at St. Petersburg many old friends and acquaintances.

I profited by the remainder of the fine weather to visit

a little of the country around St. Petersburg; for summer finishes in Russia in the month of August, and there is no autumn. I often walked in the park of Tsarskoye Selo, which is very fine and bordered by the sea; it is full of monuments that the empress calls her caprices. One sees a superb marble bridge in the style of the Palladio; Turkish baths, trophies of the victories of Romanov and Orlov; a temple with thirty-two columns, then the colonnade, and grand staircase of Hercules.

Count Cobenzl wished me much to make the acquaintance of a woman whose cleverness and beauty I had heard greatly praised, the Princess Dolgoruky. She received me with so much amiability and distinction that I at once accepted her invitation to pass a week with her. The amiable Princess Kurakin, with whom I then made acquaintance, was residing with the Princess Dolgoruky, and these two ladies with Count Cobenzl kept house together. The other guests were very numerous, and no one thought of anything but amusing themselves. After dinner we used to go in elegant boats on the river; musicians in another boat preceded us. The evening of my arrival we had a delightful concert, and the day after, theatricals. They performed the *Souterrain* by Dalayrac. The little theater was charming, and I profited by it to arrange some tableaux. I chose my personages from the handsomest men and the most beautiful women who visited us, and I draped them in cashmere shawls, of which we had an abundance. I chose serious or Bible subjects, in preference to any other. These *tableaux vivants* greatly amused the company. At the end of a week, which appeared like a moment, I bade adieu to the amiable princess; for I had made so many engagements for portraits, I could not, to my regret, stay any longer.

No woman, I believe, had ever more dignity in her person and manners than the Princess Dolgoruky; as she had seen my Sybil, which she greatly praised, she begged me to take her portrait in that character, and I had the pleasure of giving her entire satisfaction. When the portrait was completed, she sent me a very handsome carriage, and put on my arm a bracelet, made of a tress of hair, on which diamonds were arranged in such a manner that one read *Ornez celle qui orne son siècle* ("Adorn her who adorns her century"). I was extremely touched at the grace and delicacy of such a present.

As soon as Her Majesty had returned to St. Petersburg from Tsarskoye Selo, the Count Stroganov brought me an order from her to paint the two grand duchesses Alexandra and Elena. Their complexions were so fine and delicate you would have thought that they lived on ambrosia. The eldest, Alexandra, was of the Grecian type; but Elena's face expressed much more refinement. I grouped them together, holding and looking at a portrait of the empress; the costume was slightly Greek, but very simple and modest. I was therefore greatly surprised when Zubov, the favorite, told me that Her Majesty was scandalized at the manner I had dressed the two grand duchesses in my picture. I so entirely believed this unkind remark that I speedily replaced my tunics by the dresses the princesses ordinarily wore and covered their arms with long sleeves. The truth is that the empress had said nothing of the kind; for she had the goodness to assure me of this the very next time I saw her. I remember that Paul, when emperor, reproached me one day for having changed the costume that I had at first given to his daughters. I told him at once how it had occurred, on which he shrugged his shoulders and said, "It was a trick played on you."

Crowds came to my rooms to see the portraits of the grand duchesses and my other works. As I did not wish to lose all my mornings, I had fixed Sunday morning to open my studio, as I had always done in the countries I had visited. My rooms faced the palace; the carriages of all those who came to make their court to the empress had only to turn to arrive at once at my door.

Why Zubov did not like me I have never rightly been able to guess. It is possible that the favorite was ill-disposed toward me because I had seemed to neglect his patronage. Zubov liked people to ask for his support; but pride has always made me fear that people might attribute to protection the success I desired to obtain. Whether right or wrong, I wished to owe my reputation and fortune to my palette.

As soon as I had finished the portraits of the grand duchesses, the empress commanded me to take that of the Grand Duchess Elizabeth, recently married to Alexander. I have already said what an enchanting person this princess was; I should have preferred to have painted her according to my imagination, instead of in the ordinary costume of the day; but since this was not to be, I painted her full-length, in court dress, arranging flowers in a basket. When I had finished her large portrait, she made me take another for her mother, in which I painted her with a transparent violet shawl, leaning against a cushion. I can say that the more I saw of her, the more I found her manner kind and lovable. One morning, when she was giving me a sitting, a sudden giddiness seized me, my eyes seemed to be full of sparks; she became much alarmed, and ran herself to fetch me water, and bathed my eyes, caring for me with the greatest solicitude, and on my return home sent at once to inquire how I was.

Every evening I went out. Not only the balls, concerts, theaters were frequent, but I delighted in the evening parties, where I found all the urbanity and grace of French society; for to use an expression of the Princess Dolgoruky, it appeared as through good taste had bounded from Paris to St. Petersburg.

The peace and happiness I enjoyed did not prevent my thinking very often of France and her troubles. I was always pursued by the thought of Louis XVI and Marie Antoinette, so that my greatest desire was to execute a painting representing them in one of the solemn and touching moments which preceded their death. I knew that Cléry had taken refuge in Vienna, after the death of his illustrious master; I wrote and informed him of my intentions, begging him to help me in carrying them out.

Shortly after I received a letter that made such a painful impression on me that I felt it to be impossible to undertake a work when each stroke of the brush would have made me burst into tears. I therefore renounced my intentions.

The people lived so happily during the reign of Catherine that I can positively affirm having heard her blessed by both small and great, as one to whom the nation owed so much of its glory and well-being. During the space of thirty-four years, the time she reigned, her benevolent genius created or protected all that was useful and glorious. She covered the sea by her fleet and established everywhere manufactories and banks, so essential to the commerce of St. Petersburg, Moscow, and Tobolsk. She accorded new privileges to the Academy, founded schools in all the towns and country districts, built canals and raised granite quays, formed a new code of laws, and finally she introduced in her empire the blessing of vaccination. All these beneficent actions are due to Catherine alone, for she never gave any real authority to others; she dictated herself the dispatches to her ministers, who were in reality only her secretaries.

Catherine II loved whatever was grand in art. She caused to be built at the Hermitage rooms like those at the Vatican and had copied the fifty paintings by Raphael which ornament them; she also decorated the Academy with plaster models of the most beautiful antique statues and several paintings by different masters. The

Hermitage, which she had erected and placed near her palace, was a model of good taste and caused the heavy architecture of the Imperial Palace at St. Petersburg to look all the more hideous.

The Sunday preceding her death, I went the morning after the Mass to present to Her Majesty the portrait I had made of the Grand Duchess Elizabeth. The empress came toward me and complimented me about it, and then said, "They insist on your doing my portrait; I am very old, but since they desire it so much I will give you the first sitting this day week." The Thursday after, she did not ring at nine o'clock as usual. They waited till ten and even later; at last the head waiting maid entered. Not seeing the empress in her room, she went to the little clothes cupboard, and as soon as she opened the door the body of Catherine fell to the ground. The anxiety was intense, everybody felt it, for not only were they fond of Catherine but they had great dread of the reign of Paul!

Paul I, born the first of October, 1754, ascended the throne the twelfth of October, 1796. Paul was clever, intelligent, and energetic, but the originality of his character verged on madness. This unlucky prince had outbursts of kindness and generosity which were often succeeded by fits of rage, and his kindnesses or anger, his favor or displeasure, were entirely caused by some passing caprice. The slightest departure from Paul's commands was punished with exile to Siberia, or imprisonment at least, so that from never being able to tell where madness, coupled with arbitrary power, was likely to lead him, people lived in a perpetual terror. I cannot describe the terror with which Paul inspired me, and can only account for it by knowing how universal was the feeling; for I must confess that to me he was never otherwise than polite and kind.

Nevertheless, St. Petersburg was not an unpleasant residence for an artist. The Emperor Paul loved and protected the fine arts. Doyen, my father's friend and the historical painter I have already spoken about several times, was as much patronized by Paul I as he was by Catherine II. The room where Doyen worked was near the Hermitage; Paul and the whole court crossed it to go to Mass, and it was seldom that the emperor did not stop to have a chat with the painter in a most friendly manner. If my father's old friend was pleased with his fortune at St. Petersburg, I was none the less pleased with mine. I worked unceasingly from morning to evening. Only on Sundays I lost two hours, which I was obliged to give to those who wished to visit my studio; among the number were often the grand dukes and grand duchesses. Besides the paintings of which I have spoken and numerous portraits, I had procured from Paris my picture of Queen Marie Antoinette, the one in which I painted her in a blue velvet dress—the interest it caused gave me great pleasure.

Having been ordered by the emperor to paint a portrait of the empress, his wife, I represented her on foot, wearing a court dress and a crown of diamonds. I do not care to paint diamonds; the brush cannot give them sufficient brilliancy. But by making a background of a crimson velvet curtain, which brought out the crown into relief, I managed to make it as brilliant as it was possible to do. When I had the painting in my own rooms to finish it, they wished to lend me the court dress with the diamonds as well, but I refused this mark of confidence which would have made me live in a state of terror; I preferred to paint them at the palace, and had my painting carried back accordingly. Our sittings always took place after the court dinner, so that the emperor and his two sons, Alexander and Constantine, were often present. These august personages did not make me feel at all embarrassed, as the emperor, the only one I feared, was always good to me. One day he brought me my cup of coffee himself, as I was standing at my easel, waited till I had finished it, and took it away again.

One of the pleasantest memories I have is that of my reception as a member of the St. Petersburg Academy. I was informed by Count Stroganov, then director, of the day fixed on for my reception. I had ordered for myself the Academy uniform, a riding habit with a little violet waistcoat, yellow petticoat, and black hat and feathers. I made my own portrait for the Academy of St. Petersburg and represented myself painting, with my palette in my hand.

I quitted St. Petersburg feeling ill and sad, my doctor having told me I ought to drink the Carlsbad waters for my complaint. When I passed the Russian frontier, I burst into tears and made up my mind to revisit those who had for so long shown me every mark of friendliness and affection; but it was my destiny, or fate, never to see again the land which I still consider my second country.

My first stoppage was at Narva, and I reached Riga afterward. At Königsberg I took the regular postal conveyance to Berlin, which I reached toward the end of July, 1801. Three days sufficed to restore me from my fatigues, when the Queen of Prussia, who was not at Berlin, had the goodness to ask me to visit her at Potsdam, where she wished me to take her portrait. My pen is powerless to describe the impression made on me by this princess. The charm of her lovely face with its fine and regular features; her beautiful figure, neck, and arms, and the dazzling whiteness of her complexion, everything about her surpassed my expectations. She expressed a desire to see the studies I had made of the Emperor Alexander and the Empress Elizabeth, and was much satisfied with them.

On my arrival in Berlin I had paid a visit to General Beurnonville, the French ambassador, for I entertained a great desire to return to Paris. My friends and my brother, in particular, were anxious for me to do so; it had been easy for them to get me struck off the list of émigrés, and I was reestablished in my quality of French woman, to which in spite of all I still clung in my heart. A few days before my departure from Berlin, the director of the Academy of Painting came most courteously and brought me himself the diploma of my reception by this Academy.

On leaving Berlin, I went to Dresden, where I was compelled to remain in order to make several copies of the portrait of the Emperor Alexander which I had promised. I intended afterward to continue my journey to France, without stopping any length of time on the road. The following letter, which I wrote when at Dresden to my brother, will give some idea of what I felt at the time:

Dresden, September 18, 1801

It is ages, my good friend, since I wrote to you, but I have always been on the move.... The longing you have to see me is only equal to my own, but, my dear friend, I cannot conceal from you the dread I feel in returning to Paris. The remembrance of the horrors that have passed there is so vividly before my eyes that I fear to revisit the places which have been witness of such frightful scenes. I should wish to have been blind or to have drunk of the waters of oblivion, in order to live on that blood-stained soil. On the other hand, when I think of the happiness it will be to embrace you again, to meet old friends who are still left to me, I no longer hesitate, and I say to myself that I will return. . . .

I will not attempt to describe the state of my feelings on again touching, after twelve years, French soil; the terror, the sorrow, and the joy which agitated my mind in turn. I wept for friends who had died on the scaffold; but I was going to see others who still remained to me. This France into which I was entering had been the theater of atrocious crimes; but this France was my country!

On my arrival at my house in Paris, in the rue du Gros-Chenet, M. Le Brun, my brother, his wife, and daughter were waiting at the entrance door to receive me, weeping for joy at seeing me again, and I also was much overcome. The first visit I received the following morning was that of Greuze, whom I did not find changed. I was touched by his friendliness and was very glad to see him again. A few days after my arrival, Mme Bonaparte came one morning to see me; she brought to my recollection the balls we had been to together before the Revolution and which I had quite forgotten.

Ménageot soon called; he had been director of the Academy of French Painters in Rome. He told me how he had seen Bonaparte at Lodi, after his great victory. Bonaparte, on showing him the field of battle still strewn with dead, said to him with the greatest sangfroid, "This would make a fine picture."

I was greatly touched at the joy expressed by my friends and acquaintances at seeing me again, though my pleasure was sadly troubled at hearing of so many deaths of which I was ignorant; for there was scarcely anyone who called who had not lost either a mother, husband, or some relative.

One can imagine with what delight I visited the Musée du Louvre, which possessed so many splendid works of art; I went there alone, so that I might enjoy it without anything to distract me. I first visited the pictures, then the statues; and when after having remained several hours standing, I perceived that the guardians had locked up the doors and gone away. I ran right and left; I cried; it was impossible to make myself heard; I was dying of cold and hunger, for it was in the month of February. I found myself in prison with all these fine statues, which I no longer was in any disposition to admire. They appeared like so many phantoms, and the idea that I should have to pass the night with them filled me with terror and despair. At last I discovered a little door, at which I knocked so loudly that someone heard me and opened it; I ran out precipitately, delighted to regain my liberty.

The appearance of Paris was not so gay; the streets seemed narrower. But what displeased me more than anything else was to see written on the walls: *liberté, fraternité, ou la mort*. These words raised in my mind many sad reflections on the past and filled me with fears for the future.

I was taken to see a grand parade held by the First Consul on the Place du Louvre. I was stationed at a window of the museum, and I remember that I could not be made to recognize as Bonaparte the little slight man who was pointed out to me as him. As in the case of the Empress Catherine II, I had imagined this celebrated man to be a sort of colossus.

The first artist on whom I called was M. Vien, who had been appointed in the old times as first painter to the King, and whom Bonaparte had made a senator. He was then eighty-two years of age; nevertheless, he showed me two sketches composed in the style of the antique bacchanals which he had just painted. They were charming. After this visit I called on M. Gérard, already so celebrated by his pictures of Belisarius and of Psyche. I had the greatest desire to become acquainted with this splendid artist, whose quality of mind equaled his rare talent. I found him worthy of his fame. He had just finished painting the fine portrait of Mme Bonaparte, mother of the Emperor Napoleon I; she is depicted reclining on a sofa, and this picture added still more to his reputation.

The great number of foreigners of my acquaintance who were at this period in Paris, and the necessity I felt to try to drive away the melancholy which I could not overcome, induced me to give *soirées*. I collected at one of them all the principal artists of the period, and we were as gay as before the Revolution. At dessert, each person was obliged to sing a song. Gérard chose the air of "Marlborough," but, to tell the truth, his singing was not as perfect as his painting, for he sang false, and we laughed at him.

I saw nearly every day the Princess Dolgoruky, who had been so kind to me at St. Petersburg. She liked Paris; she came to see me the day she had been presented to Bonaparte. I asked her what she thought of the Court of the First Consul. "It is not a court," she replied, "but a power." It must have appeared as such to her; while at the Tuileries, she would see very few women but a prodigious number of military of all ranks.

In the midst of the distractions which a residence in Paris offered me, I was not the less haunted by the most gloomy thoughts. To put a stop to such a state of mind I resolved on taking a journey, and never having visited London, decided on going there.

I left for London on the fifteenth of April, 1802. I did not know a word of English. Great and beautiful as London is, it offers less resources for an artist than Paris or the Italian cities. It is not that England does not possess many precious works of art, but the greater number are the property of private individuals, who make them the ornament of their town or country houses. At the time of which I speak, London did not possess any museum of pictures, that which exists at the present time being the fruit of legacies and presents made to the nation within the last few years. For want of pictures, I went to see the monuments.

The walks in London are not at all gay; the women all walk together on one side dressed in white. Their silence, their perfect calm, might make one fancy they were shadows passing along. The men keep themselves apart from them and maintain the same serious appearance.

I visited nearly all the principal artists and was extremely surprised to see with all of them a quantity of portraits of which the head alone was finished. I asked them why they sent portraits in this condition to be exhibited; they all replied that the persons who had sat for them were contented to be seen and named; and besides, the sketch once made, half the price was paid in advance, and the painter was satisfied. I saw many of Sir Joshua Reynolds's famous pictures; they are a most excellent color, and remind one of Titian, but in general are unfinished with the exception of the head. The London climate greatly worried this artist, as so unfavorable for drying the paint, and he had tried mixing wax with his paints, but this he found deadened them.

Shortly after my arrival in London, the Treaty of Amiens having been broken, all the French who had not lived in England over a year were obliged to leave at once. The Prince of Wales, to whom I had been presented, assured me that I should not be included in this order.

A little before my departure from London I took the portrait of the Prince of Wales. It was nearly full-length and in uniform. Many of the English painters were furious against me when they heard I had commenced this picture, and that the prince gave me as long as I liked to finish it. The ill temper of the English painters did not confine itself to mere words. A M. M—, a portrait painter, published a pamphlet in which he treated French painting in general with much bitterness, and mine in particular. I felt obliged to take upon myself the defense of the celebrated painters whose countrywoman I was, and I wrote this gentleman a severe letter on the subject:

> Monsieur,
>
> I understand that in your work on painting you speak of the French school. As, from what is reported to me concerning your remarks, I gather that you have not the least idea of that school, I think I must give you some information that you may find serviceable. I

presume, in the first place, that you do not attack the great artists who lived in the reign of Louis XIV, such as Le Brun, Le Sueur, and Simon Vouet, and Rigaud, Mignard, and Largillière, the portrait painters. As for the artists of the day, you do the French school the greatest injustice in rating it by its achievements of thirty years ago. Since then it has made enormous strides in a genre totally different from that signaling its decline. Not, however, that the man who ruined it was not gifted with a very superior talent. Boucher was a born colorist. He had discrimination in composing and good taste in the choice of his figures. But all of a sudden, he stopped working except for the dainty chambers of women, when his coloring became insipid, his style affected; and, this example once set, all painters tried to follow it. His defects were carried to the extreme, as always happens; things went from bad to worse, and art seemed irretrievably destroyed. Then came an able painter, called Vien, whose style was simple and severe. He was appreciated by true art lovers and regenerated our school. We have since produced David, the young painter Jean-Germain Drouais—who died at Rome, aged twenty-five, just as he seemed to give promise of becoming a second Raphael—Gérard, Gros, Girodet, Guérin, and a number of others I might cite.

It is not surprising that after criticizing the works of David, which you evidently do not know at all, you do me the honor of criticizing mine, which you know no better. Not knowing the English language, I had not been able to read what you wrote about my painting, and when I was told, without being given the particulars, that you had abused me soundly, I answered that however much you might disparage my pictures, the worst you could say of them would be less than I think. I do not suppose that any artist imagines he has attained perfection, and, far from any such presumption on my part, I have never yet been quite satisfied with any work of mine. Nevertheless, being now more fully informed, and knowing that your criticism bears principally on a point that appears important to me, I believe my duty is to repudiate it in the interest of art.

Patience, the only merit you allow me, is unfortunately not one of the virtues of my character. Only, it is true that I am loath to leave my work. I consider it is never complete enough, and, in the fear of leaving it too imperfect, my conscience makes me think about it a long time and touch it up repeatedly.

It seems that my lace shocks you, although I have painted none for fifteen years. I vastly prefer scarfs, which you, sir, would do well yourself to employ. Scarfs, you may believe me, are a boon to painters, and had you used them you would have acquired good taste in draping, in which you are deficient. As for those *stuffs*, those eloquent cushions, those velvets, to be seen in my *shop*, it is my opinion that one should pay as much attention as possible to all such accessories. On this point I have Raphael as an authority, who never neglected anything of this kind, who wished everything to be explicit, to be rendered minutely—that is the language of art—even to the smallest flowers in the grass. I can, furthermore, quote the example of ancient sculpture, in which not the most trifling accessories are found neglected: the draped scarfs which lie so snugly upon nude figures, and of which mere fragments are bought by real fanciers today, the ornamentation on breastplates, the buskins, all that is carried out with perfect finish.

And now, sir, allow me to remark that the word *shop*, which term you apply to my studio, is scarcely worthy of an artist. I show my pictures without having money asked at the door. I have even, to avoid that practice, set aside one day each week for persons of good standing. I may, therefore, beg you to observe that the word *shop* is improper, and that severity never excuses a man from being polite.

I have the honor to be, etc.

This letter, which I read to some friends, remained no secret to London society.

RETURN TO PARIS, A LETTER TO COUNTESS POTOCKA FROM SWITZERLAND, AND SETTLING IN LOUVECIENNES

Though I had only intended to remain four or five months in England, I was there nearly three years, detained not merely by my pecuniary interests as a painter, but still more by the great kindness shown me.

On my return to Paris, I often visited Mme de Ségur. Her husband told me that my visit to England had greatly displeased the emperor, who said to him: "Madame Le Brun has gone to see *her friends*." Bonaparte's grudge against me was not however very strong, for a few days after having spoken in this manner, he sent M. Denon to order me to paint for him the portrait of his sister, Mme Murat. I did not dare to refuse, though I was to receive only seventy-two pounds for it, being just half the sum I was in the habit of receiving for portraits of that size. This sum was even less, on taking into consideration that I included Mme Murat's little girl in the picture. It would be impossible for me to describe all the contrarieties and torments that I underwent while painting this picture. The fact is that Mme Murat was quite ignorant that punctuality is the politeness of kings, as Louis XIV so well expressed, and who in truth was no parvenu.

Delivered from the torture caused by painting Mme Murat, I continued my tranquil way of life, but my taste for travel was not entirely sated: I had not yet seen Switzerland, so I set off in 1808 to wander through the mountains. As I wrote an exact account of this trip to Countess Potocka, I limit myself to placing here the letters which I wrote to her and of which I had kept duplicates.

LETTER VI

Dear Countess, I have just spent one week at Coppet with Mme de Staël. I had only recently finished reading her last novel, *Corinne ou l'Italie*; her sparkling and inspired personality gave me the idea of painting her as Corinne, seated on a rock, holding her lyre and dressed in the costume of ancient Greece. Mme de Staël was not exactly pretty, but the liveliness of her features compensated more than adequately for any lack of formal beauty. In order to sustain the correct facial expression, I asked her to recite some lines from a tragedy; I scarcely heard them but it enabled me to paint her with an inspired expression on her face. When she had finished reciting, I said, "Pray, continue." "But you aren't listening," she replied. "Never mind," was my response, "continue all the same." Finally she understood my motive and continued declaring passages of Corneille or Racine. I intended taking the portrait to Paris for I wanted to finish the hands there.

I met several well-known people at Coppet; the pretty Mme Récamier, the Comte de Sabran, and a young Englishman; I saw the arrival of Benjamin Constant and the Prince Augustus Ferdinand of Prussia—indeed society people were constantly coming and going; they came to see the illustrious exile, the woman whom the emperor had pursued so bitterly. Mme de Staël's two sons were then at Coppet, tutored by the German man of letters, Schlegel; her daughter was extremely pretty and although still very young had an insatiable thirst for study.

Mme de Staël was a charming and unaffected hostess whose guests were left alone in the mornings and only brought together in the evening. However one could not talk to Mme de Staël herself until after supper. Then she would walk up and down the salon holding a leafy twig in one hand; when she spoke she moved the twig about and her speech had a passion that was unique to her; it was impossible to interrupt her, for she paced up and down like an inspired actress, improvising all the while.

During my stay at Coppet, I saw the play *Sémiramis*; Mme de Staël took the part of Azéma; she acted very well in certain scenes but as a whole her performance was uneven. Mme Récamier, her friend, was frightened to death by her role as Sémiramis; M. de Sabran was not at all sure about his role as Arsace, either. I have always thought that comic and proverbial dramas are the only pieces that can survive amateur productions: tragedy never works under these conditions.

From Geneva I proceeded to Ferney to see Voltaire's house. I found it tiny and very dirty; I don't think it can have been cleaned since the great man left. The bedroom is still furnished: a portrait of Lekain still sits on the right-hand side of his bed and on the opposite wall near the window hangs pictures of Mme du Châtelet, the

Abbé Delille, and a few others. The salon leads to a terrace that looks onto the Jura Mountains, but the garden itself was in a terrible state. I was deeply saddened by this neglect. Since then the house has been bought, and the new owner has had another, larger dwelling built nearby. He takes great pains to preserve the philosopher's residence and opens it to the public. I had felt just as sad on Saint Peter's Island seeing Rousseau's house being used as a common tavern.

Yours.

Returning from Switzerland, as I had no wish to pass my summers in Paris, I bought a country house at Louveciennes, which I still inhabit. The lovely view of the Seine, with the delicious woods of Marly, and the cultivated country around Louveciennes, made me think it a sort of promised land. I was established at Louveciennes when the Allied armies advanced for the second time on Paris. I shall never forget the night of the twenty-first of March, 1814. The village had just been invaded by the Prussians, who were pillaging all the houses, and my Swiss servant Joseph himself was followed by three soldiers with atrocious faces who, sword in hand, approached my bed. Joseph made himself hoarse with saying in German that I was Swiss and ill; but, without listening to him, they commenced by taking my gold snuffbox, which lay on the table by my bedside. In short, after having made me pass four hours in the most dreadful fright, these terrible people left my house, where I could no longer remain. This was not the only time I was obliged to quit it in a similar manner. On the return of the Allies in 1815, the English visited Louveciennes. They took, among other things, a superb lacquered box, which I regretted extremely, as it had been given me at St. Petersburg by my old friend, Count Stroganov.

It was on the twelfth of April, 1814, that I had the happiness of seeing the Comte d'Artois make his entry into Paris. It is impossible to describe my feelings on this occasion; I wept for joy. The strong sense of Louis XVIII was very necessary to strengthen the restoration at this epoch, when the Bonapartists were still so numerous. At last Louis XVIII himself entered Paris, bringing pardon and peace for all; I went on to the Quai des Orfèvres to see him pass. Flags hung from every window, and the cries of "Vive le roi" were so hearty and unanimous that I was quite overcome.

As I had a great desire to see Louis XVIII, I mixed in the crowd on the Sunday reception at the Tuileries to see him pass along the gallery when he went to Mass. I was placed with all the rest in front of the windows, in such a manner that the King could see us perfectly; as soon as he perceived me, he came to me, shook me by the hand in the most amiable manner, and said many flattering things on the pleasure it gave him to see me again. The greater number of persons who came back with our princes were my own friends or acquaintances. It was very sweet, after so many years of exile, to find oneself in one's own country; but alas! this happiness was not of long duration, and even while we were rejoicing over the change, Bonaparte had landed at Cannes! I leave to politicians the task of explaining why so many virtues and so much goodness did not suffice to guard and keep their throne; my grateful heart can only regret it.

During Bonaparte's reign the large portrait I had made of the Queen was stored away out of sight in the Château of Versailles. I went one day to see it. At the Restoration this picture was once more exposed to view. It represented Marie Antoinette having near her the first Dauphin and Madame holding the Duc de Normandie on her knees. I kept at home another painting of the Queen, which I had executed in Bonaparte's time. Marie Antoinette was represented ascending into Heaven; with Louis XVI and his children seated on some clouds.

I liked Louveciennes so much that, wishing to leave some souvenir of myself, I painted for the church a Saint Geneviève, on which occasion Mme de Genlis, who knew I was engaged on this work, sent me some very pretty verses. If I gave pictures, I also received them in a most delightful manner. I had often expressed the wish that my friends would paint upon the panels of my sitting room at Louveciennes and leave me some token of themselves. One fine summer's morning, at four o'clock, during my slumbers, the Prince de Crespy, the Baron de Feisthamel, M. de Rivière, and my niece, Eugénie Le Brun, set silently to work, and at ten o'clock each one had completed his panel. My astonishment can be imagined, when on coming down to breakfast I entered my room and found it adorned with these charming paintings, besides bouquets of flowers, for it was my *fête* day. Tears came into my eyes, and that was my only way of thanking my friends.

I must now speak of the last sad years of my life, when, in a very short space of time, I saw disappear from this world the beings I loved best. I lost M. Le Brun first. It was in 1819 that I lost my daughter, and in 1820 I lost my brother. So many afflictions succeeding each other made me profoundly melancholy, and my friends counselled me to try what change of scene and traveling would do. I determined on visiting Bourdeaux. This little journey was the last I made up to the time I write this. I took up again with my usual habits and painting, which of all my distractions is the one I like best. Although I have had the misfortune to lose so many who were dear to me, I am not left quite alone. I have already spoken of Mme Rivière, my niece, who by her tender care is the joy of my life. I must also mention my other niece, Eugénie Le Brun, now Mme J. Tripier Le Franc. She gave great promise from her earliest youth of becoming a good painter, much to my delight. She has followed in my footsteps, by adopting portrait painting, in which she is very successful, owing to her eye for color, truthfulness, and knack of making a perfect likeness. They both are become my children, their care and devotion throw a charm over my existence, and it is near these beloved creatures and the friends who are still left to me that I hope to end peacefully a wandering but quiet life, laborious certainly, but honorable.

Two “Portraits à la plume”

I was keen to seek out the company of all famous artists, especially those distinguished in my own particular field. David was a frequent visitor to my house, then suddenly he stopped appearing. I met him elsewhere in society and thought I would cajole him in a friendly way on the subject. "I do not like," he said, "to be part of a hierarchy." "What?" I replied. "Do you think I treat the people from the court better than the rest? Don't you think I receive everyone with the same welcome?" He continued to insist on his point, although jokingly. "Ah," I said, laughing. "I believe you suffer from pride; it hurts you not to be a duke or a marquis. I am quite indifferent to title and am equally happy to receive all, provided they are amiable people."

From then on David never came back. He even directed the hate that he bore some of my friends toward me. This came to light later, when he procured some heavy tome written against M. de Calonne, in which the author had not forgotten to drag up all the infamous slanders of which I was the subject. This book sat permanently on a stool in David's studio and was always open to the very page upon which I was mentioned. Such wickedness was both so insidious and so childish that I would have found it difficult to believe, had I not been informed of the fact by the Duc Édouard de Fitz-James and by the Comte Louis de Narbonne, as well as others of my acquaintance, who all remarked upon it and on several occasions.

However it must be said that David loved art so much that no petty hatred could prevent him from appreciating talent wherever he saw it. After I left France, I sent the portrait of Paisiello, which I had just finished painting in Naples, to Paris. It was hung in the *Salon* beneath a portrait by David, who was evidently not satisfied with his work. Approaching my painting, he looked at it for a long time and then, turning toward some of his pupils and other companions, said, "One would think that my painting was done by a woman and the portrait of Paisiello by a man." M. Le Brun overheard him say this and reported it back to me; moreover I know that David always took the time to praise my work whenever the opportunity presented itself.

It might seem that such flattering praise for my work made me forget the personal attacks leveled at me by David, but one thing I could never forgive was his atrocious conduct during the Terror: he exercised a cowardly persecution against a large number of artists, including Robert, the landscape painter, whom he had arrested and thrown into prison with a cruelty that touched on barbarity. It would have been impossible for me to renew my acquaintance with such a man. When I returned to France, one of our most famous painters came to call upon me, and during the conversation said that David was eager to see me again. I did not reply, and as the painter was a very astute man, he understood that my silence was not of that type referred to in the saying "we who say nothing mean yes."

One day Champfort brought M. de Talleyrand to see me, although he was then Abbé de Périgord; he had a gracious face, very round cheeks, and, though lame, was nonetheless elegant and renowned for his wealth. He said little to me, apart from a few words about my paintings. I have reason to believe that he was curious to see if I lived as luxuriously and magnificently as people said and that Champfort had brought him to my home so that he could convince him of the contrary. My bedroom, the only room fit to receive visitors, was furnished in a very simple manner, as M. de Talleyrand can recall to this day along with many other people.

I don't think M. de Talleyrand ever repeated his visit, but I saw him at Gennevilliers, where he dined on several occasions with the Comte de Vaudreuil, and later after I had returned to France; he was then married to Mme Grant, a very pretty woman whose portrait I painted before the Revolution and who was the subject of a rather amusing story. M. de Talleyrand was holding a dinner party for M. Denon, who had just returned from a trip to Egypt with Bonaparte; he asked his wife to read a few pages from the famous traveler's book, for he wanted her to engage in a friendly and informed conversation with him, adding that she would find the book on his desk. Mme de Talleyrand did as he asked, but made a mistake and read rather a large section of the adventures of Robinson Crusoe; later on when they were all at table, she leaned across to Denon and said in her charming voice, "Ah! monsieur, how I have enjoyed reading the story of your travels! How fascinating it is, especially the part where you meet that poor Friday." God alone knows what Denon's reaction was to these words, let alone M. de Talleyrand's. This little anecdote quickly spread through Europe; although possibly untrue, the fact that Mme de Talleyrand was not particularly intelligent remains undisputed; yet I suppose M. de Talleyrand had enough brains for both of them.

I have decided to add here at the end of my memoirs the advice that I wrote for my niece, Mme J. Tripier Le Franc, thinking that it might also be of interest to others.

Points That Should Be Observed Before You Begin to Paint

You should always be ready half an hour before the model arrives. This helps to gather your thoughts and is essential for several reasons: 1. You should never keep anyone waiting; 2. The palette must be prepared; 3. People or business should not interfere with your concentration.

An Essential Rule

You must sit your model down, but at a higher level than yourself. Make sure that the women are comfortable, that they have something to lean against and a stool beneath their feet.

You should be as far away from your model as possible; this is the only way to catch the true proportion of the features and their correct alignment, as well as the sitter's bearing and particular mannerisms which it is essential to note; the same applies when trying to achieve an overall likeness. Do we not recognize people we know from behind, even when we cannot see their face?

When painting a man's portrait, especially that of a young man, he should stand up for a moment before you begin so that you can sketch the general outline of the body. If you were to sketch him sitting down, the body would not appear as elegant and the head would appear too close to the shoulders. This is particularly necessary for men since we are more used to seeing them standing than seated.

Do not paint the head too high on the canvas since it makes the model look too tall, though if you draw the head too low, the model will become too small; when drawing the body, take care to allow more space on the side to which the body is turned.

You should also have a mirror positioned behind you so that you can see both the model and your painting at the same time, and it should be in a place where you can refer to it all the time; it is the best guide and will show up faults clearly.

Before you begin, talk to your model. Try several different poses. Choose not only the most comfortable but also the most fitting for the person's age and character, so that the pose will only add to the likeness. Likewise for the head, which should be facing either forward or at a three-quarter turn; this adds to the resemblance, especially for the public; the mirror might also help you decide upon this point.

You should try to complete the head, or at least the basic stages, in three or four sittings; allow an hour and a half for each sitting, two hours at the most, or the models will grow bored and impatient and their expressions will change noticeably, a situation to be avoided at all costs;

this is why you should allow models to rest and aim to keep their attention for as long as possible. My experience with women has led me to believe the following: you must flatter them, say they are beautiful, that they have fresh complexions, etc. This puts them in a good humor and they will hold their position more willingly. The reverse will result in a visible difference. You must also tell them that they are marvelous at posing; they will then try harder to hold their pose. Tell them not to bring their friends to the sitting, for they all want to give advice and will spoil everything, although you may consult artists and people of taste. Do not be discouraged if some people cannot find any likeness in your portraits; there are a great many people who do not know how to look at a painting.

While you are working on the head of a woman dressed in white, drape her in a neutral-colored fabric like gray or light green, so that your gaze does not wander from the model's head; if however you wish to paint her in white, keep a little white fabric to drape around the head, for it too should receive some of the reflected light.

The background to the sitter should in general be a subtle and uniform tone, neither too light nor too dark; if the background is sky, then the rules are different and you should put something blue behind the head.

Whether you are painting in pastels or oils, you should build up from the darkest color, then paint the midtones and finally the highlights.

Always thicken the highlights and always make them

golden. Between the highlights and the midtones there is another tone not to be overlooked, which has tints of violet, blue, and green. Study Van Dyck. The midtones should be broken up and less thick than the highlights, and the highlighting on the head should emphasize the bone and muscle, the latter being weaker than the former.

Immediately after the first layer comes the flesh tone, chosen according to the complexion of the sitter; this will eventually blend with the mingling, shifting midtones.

Shadow must be strong but transparent at the same time, that is to say not a thick but a ripe tone, accompanied by a strong reddish touch in the cavities, such as the eye socket, the nostrils, and the darker, interior parts of the ear, etc. The color of the cheeks, if they are unpowdered, should have a peach tone in the hollows and a golden rose color on the more fleshy parts, the two colors merging imperceptibly with the highlights to emphasize the facial bones, which should be golden. There should always be highlights on the brow bone, the cheek bone near the nose, above the upper lip, in the corner of the lower lip, and at the top of the chin, and they should always blend in with the surrounding tones. You should take care that the highlights diminish gradually and that the most salient and consequently the brightest part is always the most luminous. On the head, the sparkling lights, both sharp and diffuse, are either in the pupil or in the white of the eye, depending upon the position of the head and the eye; these two highlights often give way to others less golden in the middle of the upper eyelid, in the middle of the lower eyelid, or at least along some part of it, according to the way light falls upon the head, then on the middle of the nose, on the bridge, and the lower lip. The sharper the nose, the finer the light should be. Never use a heavy consistency of paint on the pupils: they will look more real if they have a transparent quality. You should paint in as much detail as possible, take care not to give the sitter an ambiguous gaze, and ensure that you make the pupils round. Some people have large pupils and others small, but they are always perfectly round. The upper half of the pupil is always intercepted by the upper eyelid, but if the person is angry you will often see the whole pupil. When the eye smiles, the lower half of the pupil is intercepted and covered by the lower eyelid. The white of the eye in shadow should be a pure and pristine tone, and the midtones, although they are not quite the natural color (this is so with any object you paint), should never look gray or dirty. Sometimes the eye should reflect light from the nose and share some of its shadow. The eyelashes in the shaded part are clear and stand out bright, and this is why you should use ultramarine when painting a light part that is in shadow. Observe the eye socket, which should be darker or lighter depending on its shape. It is made up of shadows and highlights, midtones, and reflections from the nose. The eyebrow should be prepared in warm tones and one should be able to see the flesh beneath the gleam of the hairs, which should be light and delicate.

The setting of the eye is always painted in delicate blueish or violet tones, depending on the whiteness and delicacy of the skin. Take care not to be too heavy with the latter or the eye will look as though it's full of tears. For this reason, one should sometimes break into the blue tones with gold, but always cautiously.

Observe the forehead well; it is vital for a true likeness and is a very important key to the personality. When the forehead has a square but prominent bone, such as in the self-portraits of Raphael, Rubens, or Van Dyck, there is a definite concentration of light on these prominent areas. The first is at the top of the forehead, just beneath the hairline. It is then interrupted and reappears near the eyebrow. This in turn gives way to the color of the temple where there will often be a blue vein visible, especially if the sitter's skin is very fine. In between these highlights is the natural flesh tone which fades into the center. The light returns, if more feebly, on the same bone on the other side. This midtone mingles softly with all the other midtones, eventually becoming the shadow that defines the shape of the brow bone. After this shadow, there is a slightly golden reflection, depending upon the color of the hair. Above the eyebrow, the tone should become a little warmer: the accumulation of these hairs has the same effect as a mass of curls falling onto a well-lit forehead. The shadow is warm. Look at the heads of Greuze and study the way in which your model's hair grows; this will add to the likeness and the painting will be more truthful. You should observe the part where the hair falls next to the skin so that you will be able to render it as realistically as possible; there should never be a hard line between the two; the hair and the skin should mingle slightly, in form and color; this way the hair will not look like a wig, an inevitable error if one does not follow the method I have just described.

The hair should be drawn in a body and should remain as such for the most part; it is probably better to use a glaze, otherwise the colors may bleed into the shadow and the main flesh tones of the face. The highlights on the hair are only visible on the prominent parts of the head; curls reflect light in the center and a few stray hairs break the uniformity. The edge of the hair should, like metal, have something of the background color, for this helps to accentuate the turn of the head.

It is also essential to study the ear and to place it in the correct position, understanding that it is a link between the head and the neck; you should make the shape as beautiful as you can; study the art of antiquity or beautiful examples in nature. For example, you might notice how in general the Germans, and especially the Austrians, have ears that are situated a little too high according to perfect proportion. Likewise, the way the neck sits upon the shoulders is different from that of other peoples: it is wide, thick, and rises high behind the ear. These people also have very strong temple bones. So if you happen to be painting a German, you should conserve this characteristic trait, along with the prominent forehead and the usually flat, sunken cheeks. As far as possible, try to paint the complete ear and study its cartilage formation well, even if you are going to paint hair over it. The color that determines its shape should be warm and transparent, apart from the earhole, which should always be dark and opaque. Its flesh tones, even when highlighted, should in general be less luminous than the cheek, which is more prominent. The shadow thrown on the neck by the ear is very warm in daylight; the jaw should be drawn in subtle tints with delicate midtones in order to obtain the depth between jaw and neck. If the head belongs to a woman, the base of the jaw should have warmer tones than that of a man, whose beard absorbs the naturally warm flesh tones beneath. The shadow on the neck should also be very subtle and less ruddy than the face. It is essential to observe the proportion of the collarbones relative to the position of the head, as well as the way they reflect light; the chest area becomes a little deeper in color toward the point where the collarbones meet; in general the articulations, such as the elbow, the kneecap, the heel, and the knuckle, are always darker than the rest of the body.

If you have to paint breasts, put the model in a position where they are well lit; the best conditions for painting breasts occur when the light is direct, and the color should grow gradually stronger toward the nipple; the midtones which curve around the breast should be as light and fresh as possible; the shadow between the breasts should be warm and transparent.

There are rules for the gradation of light, such as I have described for the head, for the rest of the body. If the figure is seated, the light focuses strongly upon the thighs and will gradually fade toward the heel.

ÉLISABETH LOUISE VIGÉE LE BRUN (1755–1842) was a celebrated French painter at the turn of the nineteenth century and one of few women artists admitted to the Académie royale de peinture et de sculpture. She is well known for her portraits of the aristocracy and royal families, including her patron Marie Antoinette. She had contributed more than fifty pictures to the *Salons*, including history paintings and allegories, by 1789. With the outbreak of the French Revolution, she fled Paris and traveled across Europe and Russia, continuing to paint. Vigée Le Brun returned to Paris in 1802, and in 1825, settled in Louveciennes, she set out writing and publishing her memoirs.

ANNE HIGONNET is a professor of art history at Barnard College, Columbia University. She is the author of *Liberty, Equality, Fashion: The Women Who Styled the French Revolution* (2024). She has written five other books as well as many essays and has directed two book-scale digital projects. Her research has been supported by Getty, Guggenheim, Social Science Research Council, and Harvard-Radcliffe Institute Fellowships, as well as by grants from the Mellon, Howard, and Kress Foundations.

THE *EKPHRASIS* SERIES

"Ekphrasis" is traditionally defined as the literary representation of a work of visual art. One of the oldest forms of writing, it originated in ancient Greece, where it referred to the practice and skill of presenting artworks through vivid, highly detailed accounts. Today, "ekphrasis" is more openly interpreted as one art form, whether it be writing, visual art, music, or film, that is used to describe another art form, in order to bring to an audience the experiential and visceral impact of the subject.

The *ekphrasis* series from David Zwirner Books is dedicated to publishing rare, out-of-print, and newly commissioned texts as accessible paperback volumes. It is part of David Zwirner Books's ongoing effort to publish new and surprising pieces of writing on visual culture.

OTHER TITLES IN THE *EKPHRASIS* SERIES

On Contemporary Art
César Aira

Something Close to Music
John Ashbery

The Salon of 1846
Charles Baudelaire

My Friend Van Gogh
Émile Bernard

Strange Impressions
Romaine Brooks

A Balthus Notebook
Guy Davenport

Hebdomeros
Giorgio de Chirico

That Still Moment
Edwin Denby

Ramblings of a Wannabe Painter
Paul Gauguin

Thrust: A Spasmodic Pictorial History of the Codpiece in Art
Michael Glover

Visions and Ecstasies
H.D.

Mad about Painting
Katsushika Hokusai

Blue
Derek Jarman

Kandinsky: Incarnating Beauty
Alexandre Kojève

Pissing Figures 1280–2014
Jean-Claude Lebensztejn

The Psychology of an Art Writer
Vernon Lee

Degas and His Model
Alice Michel

28 Paradises
Patrick Modiano and Dominique Zehrfuss

Any Day Now: Toward a Black Aesthetic
Larry Neal

Summoning Pearl Harbor
Alexander Nemerov

Chardin and Rembrandt
Marcel Proust

Letters to a Young Painter
Rainer Maria Rilke

The Cathedral Is Dying
Auguste Rodin

Giotto and His Works in Padua
John Ruskin

Duchamp's Last Day
Donald Shambroom

Dix Portraits
Gertrude Stein

Photography and Belief
David Levi Strauss

The Critic as Artist
Oscar Wilde

Oh, to Be a Painter!
Virginia Woolf

Two Cities
Cynthia Zarin

Souvenirs
From a Memoir
Élisabeth Louise Vigée Le Brun

Published by
David Zwirner Books
520 West 20th Street, 2nd Floor
New York, New York 10011
+ 1 212 727 2070
davidzwirnerbooks.com

Editor: Elizabeth Gordon
Proofreader: Chris Peterson

Design: Michael Dyer / Remake
Production manager: Luke Chase
Color separations: VeronaLibri, Verona
Printing: VeronaLibri, Verona

Typeface: Arnhem
Paper: Holmen Book Cream, 80 gsm

Distributed in the United States and Canada by
Simon & Schuster, Inc.
1230 Avenue of the Americas
New York, New York 10020
simonandschuster.com

Distributed outside the United States and Canada by
Thames & Hudson, Ltd.
181A High Holborn
London WC1V 7QX
thamesandhudson.com

ISBN 978-1-64423-162-3

Library of Congress
Control Number: 2024949466

Printed in Italy